201

SPRING HARVEST PRAISE

DIGITAL & PRINTED SONGBOOK

Spring Harvest
Equipping the Church for action

Scan to discover Spring Harvest

What's this?

On your phone, open your barcode reader app and scan the code here. If you haven't got a barcode reader then search 'qrcode' in the App Store for your smartphone.

COPYRIGHT & PHOTOCOPYING

No part of this publication may be reproduced in any form without the permission of the copyright holder of the songs and the publisher of the songbook. Exceptions to this rule are made for holders of licences issued by Christian Copyright Licensing International, as follows:

CHURCH COPYRIGHT LICENCE/COLLECTIVE WORSHIP COPYRIGHT LICENCE:
Churches, schools and organisations holding a church or collective worship copyright licence may reproduce and store the words of the songs within the terms of their licence.

MUSIC REPRODUCTION LICENCE/COLLECTIVE WORSHIP MUSIC REPRODUCTION LICENCE:
Churches, schools and organisations holding a music reproduction licence may photocopy the words and/or music of the songs directly from this publication within the terms of their licence.

For information about these licences visit ***www.ccli.co.uk***.

FOR UK, IRELAND AND EUROPE:
Christian Copyright Licensing International Ltd.
Chantry House, 22 Upperton Road, Eastbourne,
East Sussex, BN21 1BF
www.ccli.co.uk

FOR BRAZIL:
CCLI LICENCIAMENTO DE DIREITOS AUTORAIS Ltda.
Alameda Rio Negro, 1084 - Sala 75
CEP 06454-000 Barueri, SP Brasil
www.ccli.com.br

FOR AFRICA:
Christian Copyright Licensing Africa (Pty) Ltd,
PO Box 2347, Durbanville 7551, South Africa
www.ccli.co.za

FOR USA AND CANADA:
Christian Copyright Licensing Inc,
17201 NE Sacramento Street, Portland,
Oregon, 97230 USA
www.ccli.com

FOR ASIA PACIFIC:
Christian Copyright Licensing International
PO Box 6644, Baulkham Hills BC,
NSW 2153 Australia
www.ccli.com.au

KEEPING WITHIN THE LAW

If your church musicians play direct from hymnbooks, such as this one, then the purchase price of each book pays the royalties due to copyright owners. However, if you wish to photocopy music for your musicians then you will normally need permission from the copyright owner(s). Alternatively you can obtain a Music Reproduction Licence* from CCLI which permits you to photocopy the words and music of hymns and worship songs from authorised** music publications. This licence also permits you to make customised musical arrangements for transposing instruments such as wind and brass provided the melody line remains unchanged.

* The Music Reproduction Licence is supplementary to the Church Copyright Licence, i.e. your church must hold both licences.

** An Authorised book is one which is covered by the Music Reproduction Licence. NB: Both the publication containing the song you wish to photocopy and the song itself must be covered by the Music Reproduction Licence.

For more information, contact CCLI on +44 (0)1323 436103 or visit www.ccli.co.uk.

UNAUTHORISED PHOTOCOPYING IS ILLEGAL and detrimental to the work and ministry of the songwriters and publishers.

Prayers and liturgy have copyright details shown beneath them. They may be reproduced for local use with the indication of copyright, but not for resale without permission.

ACKNOWLEDGEMENTS

Music type-setting and new arrangements by David Ball
Guitar chord pages by David Ball
Songbook cover design & CD-Rom artwork by Beatroot Media
Songbook internal design & layout by Ascent Creative
Printed by Halcyon
CD-Rom authored by Cambron Software

Published & distributed by Elevation, 14 Horsted Square, Uckfield, East Sussex, TN22 1QG, UK.

Part of the Memralife Group, Registered Charity number 1126997, a Company limited by guarantee, registered in England and Wales, number 6667924. Registered Office: 14 Horsted Square, Uckfield, East Sussex, TN22 1QG.

Spring Harvest wishes to acknowledge and thank the following people for their help in the compilation and production of this songbook:

Pete Broadbent, Andrew Crookall, Jaqs Graham, Denise Hooper, Cheryl Jenkinson, Phil Loose, Sue Rinaldi, Dan Wheeler and Rachel Whitney.

Thank you to Marie Birkinshaw and Nick Harding for liturgy contributions, and Andy Smith for the MRL logo.

Special thanks to Brenda Cameron and all at Cambron Software for Power Music Lite and your help in developing this resource.

Special thanks to Jonathan Brown, Ryan Dunham, Les Moir and Adrian Thompson at Integrity Music.

ISBN 978-1-899788-88-0

CONTENTS

DISCOVER

THE SPRING HARVEST **DIGITAL SONGBOOK**

Over the years of the Spring Harvest songbook, there have been many helpful guest comments made which help us to refine our resource and hopefully deliver something more useful the following year. The one problem we've always struggled to solve is when a worship leader wants to play the song in a **different key to the book**. This may be because they need to sing it in a different register for male or female voice, or just drop it up or down a key to make it easier to lead. It may be that we want some songs to flow in a medley and to have them in the same key may help this to work.

Once again, we are very excited to partner with Power Music and bring you the Digital Songbook version of the Spring Harvest 2013 Songbook featuring the ability to **change the key of the guitar chords for every song**. Note that the music scores cannot be changed; maybe we'll be able to achieve this in the future!

Any of the songs can be printed out for your worship team or by utilising the software directly from a PC you can use monitor screens as "digital" music stands. You can build playlists for your church service, **search the songs by title, first line, Scripture or theme** and also ensure that everyone is playing in the same key. Add annotations, highlights and sticky notes to the songs, just as if you were writing on a paper book! By going online you can see just how easy it is to use the Digital Songbook powered by Power Music Lite. We recommend that you upgrade from within the Songbook to the full version as this enables you to add your own songs, purchase other songs from Power Music Store and use Cloud storage for all your songs and playlists.

new for 2013 NOW get all your 2013 songs on your iPad using the FREE Power Music app.

To see the software working go to **www.springharvest.org/digisongbook** where you can see short videos to help get to grips with the software. As with all new software expect a small learning curve, but the intuitiveness of the software makes it easy to use and makes a huge difference to both worship preparation as well as 'live' worship leading.

Presently this software is Windows PC based but for Mac users we have also packaged the song scores and guitar chords as PDFs.

If you have any support issues on the programme, email Power Music on **info@cambronsoftware.co.uk**

ALPHABETICAL & KEY INDEX

Song titles differing from first lines are in italics

SPRING HARVEST 2013

THE SOURCE

ENCOUNTERING JESUS TODAY

1

A stirring cry, an ever-fleeting breath

(Be my hope)

Key = B♭

Capo 3 (G)

Nathan Jess

♩ = 80

Chorus
Eb(C) Bb(G) F(D) Gm7(Em7) Eb(C) Bb(G) Gm7(Em7) Eb(C) Bb(G)
Je - sus, on - ly Je - sus, Je - sus be my hope! Je - sus,
D.S. for last chorus repeat (al Coda)
Last time to Coda
1. D.C.(v.3)
2.
F(D) Gm7(Em7) Eb(C) F(D) Cm9(Am9)
on - ly Je - sus, Je - sus be my hope! 3. How
Mid section
F(D) Cm9(Am9) Bb(G) F/A(D/F#)
For we have heard the cry, we've seen the hea - vy load,
2nd time D.S.
F(D) Cm9(Am9) Bb(G) F/A(D/F#)
so we must live our lives to bring this sto - ry hope!
Coda
Bb6(G6) Eb2(C2)
PHOTOCOPY THIS LEGALLY
WITH AN MRL LICENCE
FROM CCLI.CO.UK

2

All I want is you

(All I want)

Key = Bm

Jules Burt, Paul Oakley & Sam Cox

G
D
– my love, my ev - 'ry-thing. You're all I want, you're
3rd time to Coda 1 ⊕
Last time to Coda 2 ⊕⊕
G
all I need; Je - sus, my love, my ev - 'ry-thing.
1.
D.C. (v.2)
D A7 Bm A D A7 Bm A
2. Bridge
Bm D Bm
All my streams are found in you, so my soul cries out for the
1. G
2. G Bm
liv - ing God. liv - ing God. So my soul cries out for the

D.S. al Coda 1
Asus4
A
liv - ing God.
You're
Coda 1 Mid section
D
I'm pres-sing in 'cause I want to know you more, On-ly you can sa-tis-fy my soul.
Asus4
D/F♯
I'm pres-sing in 'cause I want to know you more,
1.
G
On-ly you can sa-tis-fy my soul.
2.
G
D.S. al Coda 2
You're
Coda 2
D

As I go

(Run)

♩ = 76

Key = C

Andy Smith

Verse
(v.2)
C G F C G F C
1. As I go through the cor - ri - dor of wa - ter, a new ho - ri - zon now is what I see. As I go, these walls are ris - ing high - er, the mi - ra - cle now sur - round - ing me.
'cos no - thing stands a - gainst me, there's no - thing now that's stand - ing in my way. Yeah, I'll go, with the song of o - ver com - ers. I'm sing - ing at the dawn of a new day.

Bridge
Dm7
Am7
Cap - ti - vi - ty it lies be - hind me, and
(After Mid section)
F
G
Chorus
C
free - dom is the road I'm trav - 'ling on. So I'll run
(1st D.S. D/F♮)
C/E
Fmaj7
run to my Sa - viour, run, with all that's with - in me, run,
Last time to Coda
Am7
C
F
G/F
there's no more chains that bind me now.
I'm liv - ing in you free - dom now.
1.
D.C. (v.2)
Fmaj7
2.
D.S.
Fmaj7
G/F
3.
Fmaj7
F
2. So I'll go
So I'll run

Mid section
(4th time)
(4 times, building)
G
Am7
Fmaj7
('Cos) I'm leav - ing all the chains be - hind.
Am
C
C/E
Fmaj7
D.S. al Coda
Am7
C
Fmaj7
So I'll run
Coda
Fmaj7
F
Am
NEED A COPY?
NEED AN MRL LICENCE
FROM CCLI.CO.UK!

4

As I live my life today

(Because of the cross)

Key = Bm

Lyrics: Cath Woolridge
Music: Rachel Mathias

Asus4 A
Chorus 𝄋 D A
all.
head.
Be - cause of the cross, be - cause of the blood,
Bm G D/A
free - dom gets un - der my skin. A soul syn - chro - nised to
G/B D/F♯
1.,3.,5.
Asus4 A
Christ, I'm a - live, no lon - ger caged in by my sin. Be -
2.,4.,6.
Asus4 A
(Small notes 3rd time)
1.,3.
D
sin. Be - cause of the cross.
G D
Last time to Coda 𝄌
G
D.C. (v.2)

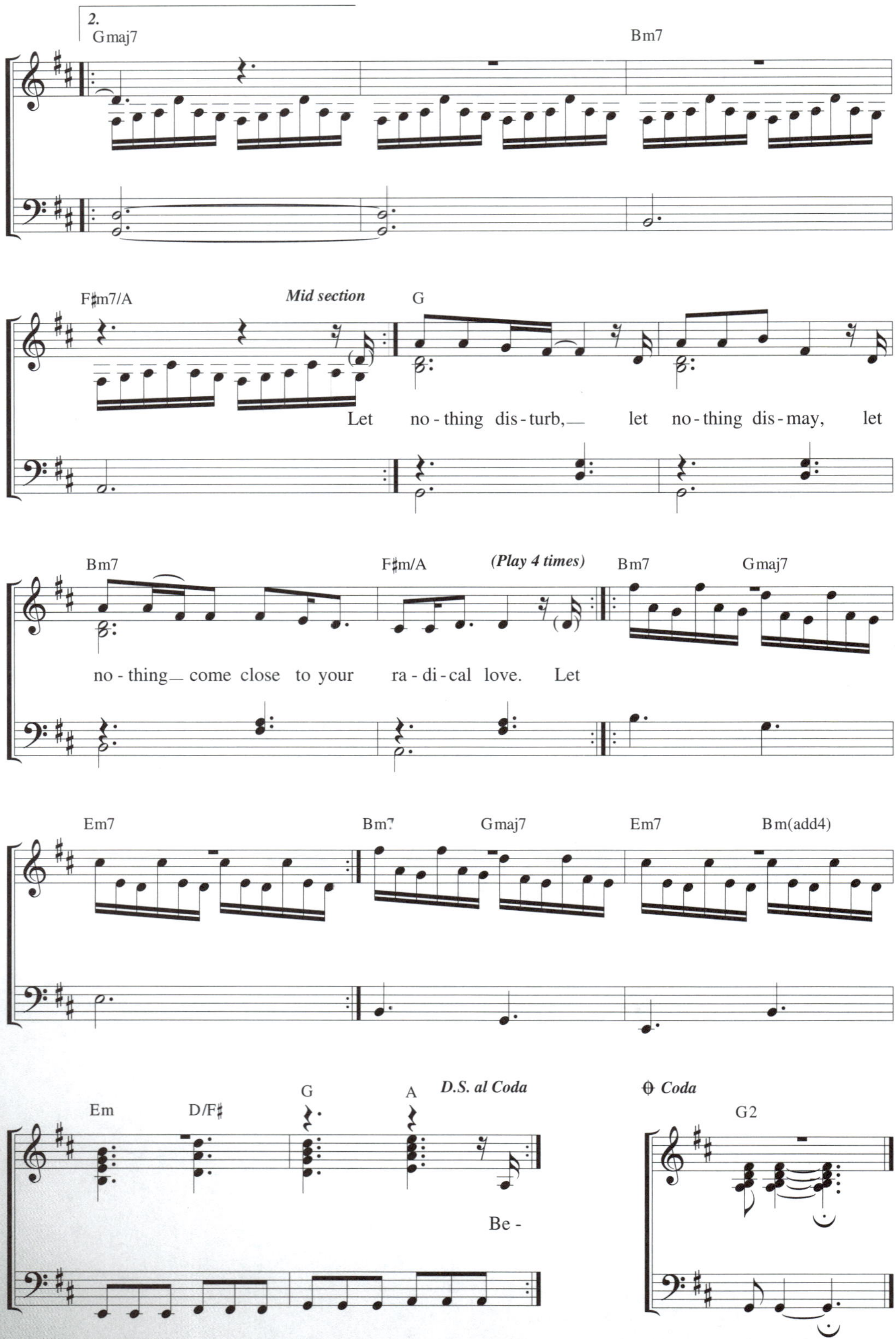
2.
Gmaj7
Bm7
F♯m7/A
Mid section
G
Let no-thing dis-turb, let no-thing dis-may, let
Bm7
F♯m/A
(Play 4 times)
Bm7
Gmaj7
no-thing come close to your ra-di-cal love. Let
Em7
Bm7
Gmaj7
Em7
Bm(add4)
Em
D/F♯
G
A
D.S. al Coda
Be -
Coda
G2

Bless the Lord, O my soul

(Better than life)

5

Capo 3 (D)

Key = F

♩ = 126

Vicky Beeching

Dm7(Bm7) C(A) B♭(G) F(D)
make my heart light. Here in your pre - sence is
3rd time D.S.S. al Coda
Last time to Coda
Dm7(Bm7) C(A) Gm7(Em7) E♭(C)
full - ness of joy, so I'll dance and I'll sing, for you are my ev - 'ry - thing.
1st time D.C. (v.2)
B♭2(G2) F(D) Dm7(Bm7) C(A) B♭2(G2) F(D) Dm7(Bm7) C(A)
Mid section
F(D) C/E(A/C♯) B♭2/D(G/B)
A - maz - ing grace how sweet the sound, I once was lost
F/A(D/F♯) F(D) B♭2(G2) Am7(F♯m7) Gm7(Em7)
but now I'm found, I once was blind but now I see; thank you for

1.
C7(A7)
2.
C7(A7)
D.S. (v.1)
lov - ing me.
lov - ing me.
I will not for -
Coda
B♭2(G2) F(D) Dm7(Bm7) C(A) B♭2(G2) F(D)
You are my ev - 'ry - thing.
Dm7(Bm7) C(A) B♭2(G2) F(D) Dm7(Bm7) C(A)
You are my ev - 'ry - thing.
B♭2(G2) F(D) Dm7(Bm7) C(A) F(D)

6 Come set your rule and reign

(Build your Kingdom here)

Key = D

♩ = 134

Rend Collective Experiment

A G D A G D A
We are your church, we need your pow'r in
We are your church, we pray: "re - vive this
— we are your church, we are the hope on
1. D Dsus4 D.C.(v.2)
2. D Dsus4
us. 2. We earth".
D Dsus4 Jump to 𝄋
3. D Dsus4 D
Build your earth. Build your
𝄋 Chorus
A Bm G D A
King - dom here, let the dark - ness fear; show your migh - ty
Bm G D/F♯ A D A Bm
hand, heal our streets and land.— Set your church on fire, win this

Last time to Coda
G D A Bm 1. G D/F♯
na - tion back; change the at - mos - phere, build your King - dom
A D Dsus4 D Dsus2
here we pray.
D Dsus4 D D.C.(v.3) 2. G A D A
3. Un - King - dom here we pray.
D A Bm A/C♯ Bm A/C♯ D A D D/F♯ Bm A
Bm A/C♯ D A/C♯ D D/F♯ G D/F♯ G A Bm A

OPENING PRAYER

(based on 1 John 1:1-3)

In this time of worship,
We open our eyes to see Jesus, the Way, the Truth and the Life,
We open our ears to hear Jesus, the Word of God, the Word of Life,
We open our hands to pray to Jesus, the Redeemer and transformer of Life,
Lord, we ask that today you will touch our lips,
that we might proclaim you, Jesus, the Eternal Life.

7

Come, join the celebration

(Hallelujah, what a morning)

Key = C

♩ = 136

Don Poythress,
Sue C Smith & Kenna West

1.,3.,5.,7.
2.,4.,6.,8.
F G F
has con - quered the po - wer of the grave.
that's dawn - ing,
hal - le - lu - jah,
Last time to Coda
1.
G C G
what a mor - ning.
Am B♭
D.C. (v.2)
(Women)
Ha - le - lu - jah,
Hal - le - lu - jah.
2.
Mid section
C F G Am
(Men)
Hal - le - lu - jah,
hal - le -
hal - le - lu - jah.
G/B F G
(All)
lu - jah.
Hal - le - lu - jah,
hal - le -

Am
G
D.S.
lu - jah, hal - le - lu - jah.
Coda
C
G
Hal - le - lu - jah, what a mor - ning.
Am
F
Dm7
F
F/A
G7sus4
Hal - le - lu - jah, what a mor - ning.
C

2013
THE SOURCE
22 NEW SONGS FOR THE CHURCH
Spring Harvest

8

Covered in shame, hiding my face

Key = D

(Waste it all)

Chris McClarney, Laura Rhinehart
& Christa Black

A
F♯m7
G2
to my de - fence; this price - less gift you gave was not meant
- ces fade a - way. I will spend all my days giv - ing back
D
A
Bm
Chorus
for me to hold.
the love you gave.
1. I want to waste
2. I'm gon - na waste
G
D
A
it all on you, I want to pour my heart's per - fume;
it all on you, I'm gon - na pour my heart's per - fume;
Bm
G
D
Last time to Coda
and I don't care if I'm called a fool, I'm wast - ing it all
and I don't care if I'm called a fool, I'm wast - ing it all.

1.,3.
2° D.S.S. al Coda
D.C.(v.2)
A
Bm
D
G
on you.
2.
A
Mid section
G2
oh.
All for love, and all for me, you gave
A
Bm7
it all for me to be a-live in you and you in me. Lord,
D
G2
I sur-ren - der to your love and to your touch, to
A
3
Bm7
the way you give too much; I'm too in love to not be all for you.

We just had to record this song for "The Source: New Songs for the Church"!

9 Each day I will continually praise

(Your mercy endureth)

Key = E

♩ = 130

Noel Robinson
& Michelle John

1.
2.,3.
A/E E F♯m7/E E F♯m7/E E
Bridge
in me de-clares your name. 2. O Ho - to-ry.
rit leads us to vic -
some-thing new each and ev - 'ry day.
So I sing
G A Bsus4
and I dance, where e - ver I am I will shout
B
Chorus
A E/G♯ A E
it. You are good all of the time,
A C♯m Bsus4 B A E/G♯
and your mer - cy en-dur - eth. You are good
B A C♯m Bsus4 B
all of the time, and your mer - cy en-dur - eth for-e -

1.
D.C.(v.3)
E
ver.
3. From the ris -
3.
Jump to 𝄋𝄋
2.
E
A/E E F♯m7/E E
- ver.
Not one min - - ver.
A/E E F♯m7/E E
Em7
A
Play 4 times, vocal last time
Not one min -
Mid section
𝄋𝄋
Em7 A Em7 A
- ute,
not one ho - ur,
Em7 A
not one day
with - out your po -

MEETING JESUS

We have come to meet with you,
come, Lord Jesus, and move among us.
We have come to be quiet,
come, Lord Jesus, and move within us.
We have come to praise,
come, Lord Jesus, and move our spirits.
We have come to be challenged,
come, Lord Jesus, and move our minds.
We have come to leave refreshed,
come, Lord Jesus, and move among us.

10

Even when the waters rise

(Kingdom come)

Key = Bm

Beth Croft

D.C. (v.2)
2.
G
Bm
G
2. Stand-ing
Bm/D♯
A
Mid section
Bm
To be thrown in - to flames
To see suf - f'ring and pain
G
1.,3.
Bm/F♯
Asus4
A
and still to say: my God he saves, my God he saves.
and still to say:
2.,4.
Bm/F♯
2nd time D.S.(with repeat) al Coda
A
my God he reigns.

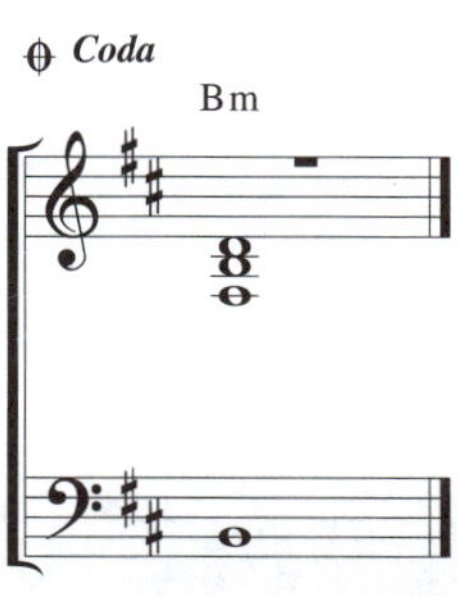
Coda
Bm

11

Faith is rising in this place

(Faith is rising)

Key = D

Nathan Fellingham

(alt chords D.S.)
Chorus
D (F♯m/D) F♯m7 (Bm/D) Bm (G/D) G
Grace is fall - ing down, there's po - wer here to heal.
D (F♯m/D) F♯m7 (Bm/D) Bm (G/D) G D
yes the time is now, God is
Last time to Coda
F♯m7 Bm G D/F♯
here with us, his Spi - rit now to heal, mer - cy
1.
A Em7 Bm D G
fall - ing down.
D.C.
Bm D G

There's a really great acoustic version of this song on "The Source: New Songs for the Church"

Father of heavenly lights

(Trust you)

12

Capo 4 (G)

Key = B

Aaron Keyes, Pat Barrett
& Matt McMichael

Chorus
E(C)
F♯(D)
B(G)
for I will, e - ver trust you
more, Lord, I will, e - ver trust you
F♯(D)
G♯m(Em)
Je - sus, trust you Je - sus, trust you
Last time to Coda
1. D.C. (v.2)
2.,4.
D.S.
E(C)
with my life. I will
3.
Mid section
E(C)
Let not the wise trust in their wis-dom,
F♯(D)
1.
E(C)
let not the strong boast in their might, let not the rich

We had a great time recording this song for "The Source: New Songs for the Church"

13

For every wounded and broken soul

(Heaven come down (This is your Kingdom come now))

Key = F

Capo 3 (D)

♩ = 78

Casey Corum, Angie Corum, Anabeth Morgan & Abigail Corum

Last time to Coda 2
F(D)
C(A)
Dm7(Bm7)
B♭(G)
hea - ven come down, hea - ven come down.
hea - ven come down, hea - ven come down.
hea - ven come down, this is your King - dom come now.
F(D)
C(A)
Dm7(Bm7)
B♭(G)
For those en - slaved by the wic - ked - ness of man we cry
For ev - 'ry fam - 'ly that's been torn a - part we cry
Our bro - ken bo - dies are be - ing made whole, this is
F(D)
C(A)
Dm7(Bm7)
B♭(G)
hea - ven come down, hea - ven come down.
hea - ven come down, hea - ven come down.
hea - ven come down, this is your King - dom come now.

F(D) C(A) Dm7(Bm7) B♭(G)
For the hea - vy - la - den, weighed down by sin we cry
For the sin - gle mo - ther with a bro - ken heart we cry
As way - ward chil - dren, we find our way home, this is
v.3 only
F(D) C(A) Dm7(Bm7) B♭(G)
hea - ven come down, let your
hea - ven come down, let your
hea - ven come down, this is your King - dom come now. This is
F(D) C(A) Dm7(Bm7) B♭(G)
King - dom come now.
King - dom come now.
hea - ven come down, this is your King - dom come now.

Dm7(Bm7)
C(A)
Chorus
Dm7(Bm7)
B♭(G)
F(D) Dm7(Bm7)
Send us out to be your hands and feet,
C(A)
Dm7(Bm7)
B♭(G)
Dm7(Bm7)
F(D)
C(A)
Last time to Coda 1
A/C♯(F♯/A♯)
al-ways search-ing for the lost and the least.
Send your po-wer, set the
(last time) set your
Dm7(Bm7)
Gm7(Em7)
F/A(D/F♯)
1.
D.C. (v.2)
Csus4(Asus4)
3.
D.S. al Coda 1
C(A)
Dm7(Bm7)
peo-ple free, and let your King-dom come.
come.
2.
Csus4(Asus4)
Gm7(Em7)
F/A(D/F♯)
C(A)
Mid section
come, and on earth your will be done.
Oh,
D♭(B♭)
E♭(C)
F(D)
D♭(B♭)
E♭(C)
oh,

F(D) D♭(B♭) E♭(C) F(D)
oh. Lord, won't you come,
2nd time D.C. (v.1) al Coda 2
E♭(C) B♭(G) D♭(B♭) E♭(C)
Lord won't you come, Lord, let your King - dom come on earth.
(omit 2nd time)
F(D) D♭(B♭) E♭(C)
Lord let your po - wer fill our hearts.
F(D) D♭(B♭) E♭(C)
Lord let your King - dom come through us.
F(D) E♭(C) B♭(G)
D.C.(v.3)
Lord won't you come, Lord won't you come.

Coda 1
Dm7(Bm7) Gm7(Em7) Gm7(Em7) F/A(D/F♯)
peo - ple free, and let your King - dom
Csus4(Asus4) C(A) Gm7(Em7) F/A(D/F♯)
1. Csus4(Asus4) C(A)
2. D.S.S. Csus4(Asus4)
come, and on earth your will be done. Lord, done. Oh,
Coda 2
Dm7(Bm7) B♭(G) F(D) C(A)
hea - ven come down. We cry hea - ven come down, let your
Dm7(Bm7) B♭2(G2)
King - dom come now.

14

From the highest throne

(Endless light)

Key = C

♩ = 114

Dean Ussher
& Karl Cashwell

1.
D.C.(v.3)
C
Gsus4
G
C
sing your praise.
sing your praise.
2.,4.
D.S. ch.2
3.,5.
Mid section
G
G
F
2. Hope of
God be ex-al-ted, God be ex-al-ted
Last time to Coda
Am
G
F
Am
G
in ev-'ry-thing. We live for your glo-ry, live for your glo-ry.
1.,2.,4.
3.
D.S. ch.1
C
1. Lord of
Coda
C
Csus4
C
Csus4
C

15 God of mercy, full of grace

(Hear the sound)

Key = C

♩ = 104

David Leonard, Leslie Jordan
& Matt Maher

Dm
Am
F
Gsus4
Last time to Coda
of your ma - je - sty,
Lord hear the sound,
1.
G
C
F/C
C
Gsus4
G
Lord, hear the sound.
D.C.
F
2.,4.
G
D.S. (al Coda)
3.
G
So let the hea - ven's roar
Lord, hear the sound.
F
Bridge
G
Am
Ev - 'ry - one,
ev - 'ry - one,
F
G
Am
F
Mid section
ev - 'ry - one
ev - 'ry - one.
Ev - 'ry - one

G
Am
you for-give, you for - give. Ev - 'ry - one you re-store, you re -
F
G
1.
C
store. Ev - 'ry - one you re-deem you re - deem, ev - 'ry - one.
2.
Fmaj7
D.S.
Ev - ry - one - deem, ev - 'ry - one. So let the hea - ven's roar
Coda
G
C
F/C
C
Lord, hear the sound.
Gsus4
G
F
C

MARTIN SMITH WRITES...

When I was a young teenager I remember my parents talking about this event called Spring Harvest. Apparently there would be 'cool' meetings just for kids, a swimming pool and a rock band leading the hymns. We were part of a small 100 strong Brethren assembly in Essex and so seeing a drum kit playing in church was not a common experience!

I can remember the moment vividly when mum and dad allowed me to go to the big top one night. I think that moment changed my life forever. There on stage I saw people with electric guitars, trumpet players, weird looking electric pianos and this guy singing with a ginger beard. I found out his name was Graham Kendrick. I remember he had a rainbow guitar strap and even then I couldn't decide whether it was hip or cheesy but I LOVED it. I can remember the sound. The sound of 5000 saints singing their hearts out to Jesus. "Shine Jesus shine", I could feel the power of praise, worship, belting out songs together. I decided then and there that whatever the guy at the front was doing, I wanted to do the same. Many years later I met Graham. He has been a faithful father figure to me and many of his worship 'kids' who have grown up in the UK.

Years later God gave me the chance to be a part of an amazing move of God across the world. We took that sound I felt and heard when I was 12 and turned it up a bit louder. It needed to be loud to cut through the noise of a confused, post modern, post Christian culture happy to believe that God was dead and Jesus was merely a 'good' guy. Delirious? was our name, and like the dictionary definition we were 'wildly excited' about God, seeing a generation give their lives away and wanting to be Historymakers wherever they were. Praying for our nations to be changed with the Glory of God. The band came to an end in 2009 and a period of transition for me began into the unknown, into a new future.

Being off the road for a time was good. Time to reconnect with my soul, with my family, with God. Time to listen to him, to lay it all down and trust that he had a plan.

Around this time someone showed me a YouTube clip of Jesus Culture singing 'He loves Us'. I was deeply impacted by it. I knew there was something fresh about it, they had a connection with God that I knew I'd lost a bit. We met up, lead worship at a conference, which lead to playing together in New York and making a live record together. It was awesome. To be on stage with them was incredible and the evenings of worship were unforgettable.

I'm very grateful too that I have the chance to put out some new music, to encourage the church to keep dancing. If we stop dancing then we lose the joy of our salvation and church should be the most joyful place there is.

Music in church shouldn't be dull, or formulaic but it should be explosive. Reflecting the love and majesty of our living God. We must remember that he is NOT dead but alive and we have everything to celebrate.

It doesn't matter where you've come from, just matters that you're here. See you all on God's great dance floor.

Martin Smith
www.martinsmith.tv

16

God you are my God

Key = Am

Worshipfully ♩ = 78

Pete James

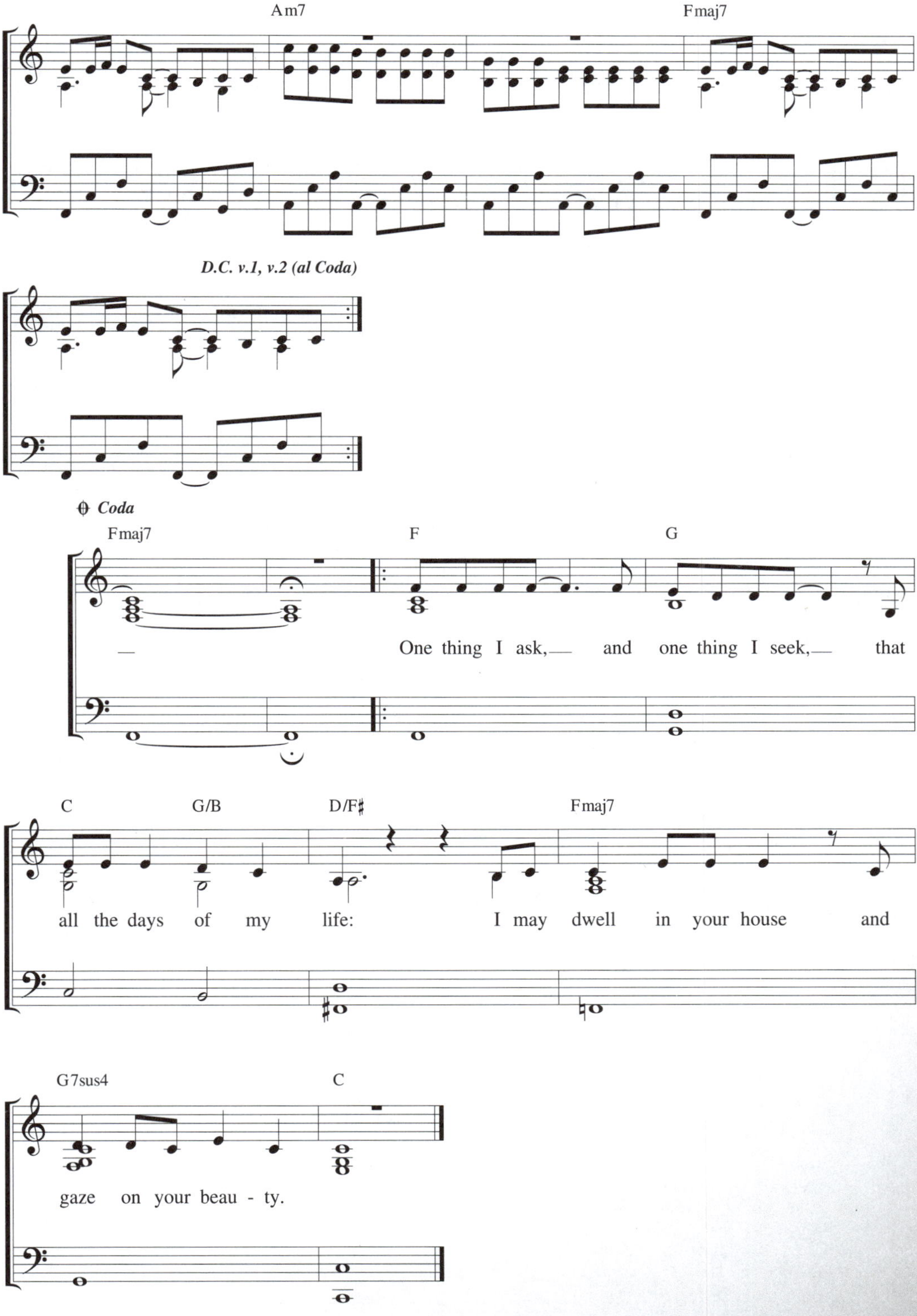
Am7
Fmaj7
D.C. v.1, v.2 (al Coda)
Coda
Fmaj7
F
G
One thing I ask, and one thing I seek, that
C
G/B
D/F♯
Fmaj7
all the days of my life: I may dwell in your house and
G7sus4
C
gaze on your beau - ty.

17 God you are my shepherd

(You anoint my head with oil)

Capo 3(G)

Key = B♭

Rock ♩ = 94

Ruth Mayhew,
Ann & Tim O'Hare

(Small notes vv.3&4)
E♭7(C7)
(v.4)
It stret-ches out___ be-fore___ me, you bring life a-gain and a-gain.__
I'll turn my back on my fe - ars, your pre-sence makes me feel___ se-cure.__
I'll eat my fill at your ta - ble, in the pre-sence of my e - ne-mies.__
F7(D7)
Chorus
B♭7(G7)
B♭7/D(G/B)
E♭7(C7)
__ You a - noint my head with oil, And my cup___ o - ver-flows.__
B♭7(G7)
B♭7(G7)
B♭7/D(G/B)
E♭7(C7)
Last time to Coda
__ You a - noint my head with oil, my cup___ o - ver-flows.__
1.,3.
1st time D.S. (v.3)
3rd time D.S.S. (Ch repeat)
2.
B♭7(G7)
B♭7(G7)
Gm(Em)
Mid section
__ (3° You an -) __ Sure-ly good-ness and mer -
E♭7(C7)
B♭(G)
- cy will fol-low me___ all the days of___ my life.__

Gm(Em)
E♭7(C7)
F7♯9(D7♯9)
Oo yeah, good-ness and mer - cy, all o-ver me all
(Ad-lib instrumental break)
B♭7(G7)
E♭7(C7)
o-ver my life.
B♭7(G7)
E♭7(C7)
F7(D7)
D.S. (v.4)
Coda
F7♯9(D7♯9)
B♭7(G7)

God, I look to you

Capo 4 (G)

Key = B

♩ = 136

Jenn Johnson
& Ian McIntosh

C♯m7(Am7) F♯sus4(Dsus4) F♯(D) E(C)
my strength, and I will love you Lord
C♯m7(Am7) F♯sus4(Dsus4) F♯(D) B/D♯(G/B) E(C) B/D♯(G/B)
my shield, and I will love you
C♯m7(Am7) B(G) F♯/A♯(D/F♯) B(G) E(C)
Lord my rock for - e - ver, all my days I will
F♯sus4(Dsus4) B(G)
Tag
love you God. Hal - le -
E(C) C♯m7(Am7) F♯sus4(Dsus4) E(C)
lu - jah, our God reigns. Hal - le - lu - jah,
(Small notes 2nd time onwards)

C♯m7(Am7)
F♯sus4(Dsus4)
B/D♯(G/B)
E(C)
C♯m7(Am7)
our God___ reigns. Hal - le - lu - jah, our God
F♯/A♯(D/F♯)
B(G)
E(C)
F♯sus4(Dsus4)
B(G)
reigns___ for - e - ver, all___ my___ days, hal - le - lu - jah.___
To repeat (building)
Last time
B/D♯(G/B)
Hal - le

my help
comes
from the
LORD
the maker of
heaven
& earth
PSALM
121:2

19 Grace, you've shown me grace

(You have won me)

Key = A

Brian Johnson,
Jeremy Riddle & Joel Taylor

1. D.C. (v.2)
3. D.S.
E D A E E
thy of glo-ry and praise.
2.,4. (2nd time jump to Mid Section)
E D A E D A
Mid section
E D A E Bm7
Shout it out and lift up one voice in wor-ship,
D A E D/F♯ D A
sing it out un-til all the earth can hear it; Je-sus is a-live and he saves,
(Fine)
2nd time D.S.
E A/D A E
he res-cues and saves.

COPYING IT?
CCLI IT!

20

Hallelujah, hallelujah

(Emmanuel)

Key = F

Capo 2 (D)

Cathy Burton

D.C.
Dm7(Bm7)
Am7(F♯m7)
C(A)
know our ev-'ry hour, you are God with us.
Coda
B♭(G)
C(A)
Dm(Em)
Em-ma - nu-el, Em-ma - nu-el,
C(A)
Dm7(Bm7)
Em-ma - nu-el, Em-ma - nu-el,
Am7(F♯m7)
C(A)
Em-ma - nu-el, Em-ma - nu-el.
F(D)

21

Hallowed be your name

Key = C, D♭, D

Noel Robinson

♩= 90
C Dm7 G/D Csus2/E C/E C/G C Fmaj7
1. Hal - low - ed be your name, hal - low - ed
G/F Em7 Am7 Gm C7 Fmaj7 G/F
be your name. All glo - ry ho - nour and
Em Em7/B Am7 D9 Csus4/G G
1. C F G Repeat v.1
po - wer to your pre - cious ho - ly name.
2. C A♭7 D♭ E♭m7 A♭/E♭
name. 2. We lift up ho - ly
D♭sus2/F D♭/F D♭/A♭ D♭ G♭maj7 A♭/G♭ Fm7 B♭m7
hands, we lift up ho - ly hands.

A♭m D♭7 G♭maj7 A♭/G♭ Fm Fm7/C B♭m7
With a bro - ken and con - trite spi - rit, we
E♭9 D♭sus4/A♭ A♭ D♭ A♭/D♭ G♭ A♭ D♭ A♭/D♭
lift up ho - ly hands.
G♭ A♭ D A/D D G A D
3. We give prai - ses
Em7 A/E Dsus2/F♯ D/F♯ D/A D Gmaj7 A/G
to your name, we give praise to your ho - ly
F♯m7 Bm7 Am D7 Gmaj7 A/G F♯m F♯m7/C♯
name. Thy King - dom come, thy will be

Bm7 E9 Dsus4/A A D A/D D A/D
done; give prai - ses to your name.
D A/D D G♯dim C♯ F♯m7
Thy King - dom come, thy will be
Bm7 E9 Dsus4/A A
1. D G D/F♯ Em D
done; give prai - ses to your name. Thy
2. D
name.

Spring Harvest
BACK TO THE SOURCE
30 CHALLENGES TO BE, SAY, AND DO LIFE THE JESUS WAY
(WHEN YOU ARE NOT THE SON OF GOD AND SAVIOUR OF THE WORLD)
KRISH KANDIAH
"You want to be just like Jesus, because this is the way he made you. Like clay awaits a potter. Like canvas awaits a painter. Our lives long to be shaped by Jesus."
Go deeper into the Spring Harvest theme with Krish Kandiah
Available from EssentialChristian.com or your local Christian bookstore
essential christian

22

Here I am
(I give myself away)

Key = Bb

Capo 3(G)

Gospel feel ♩ = 62

Sam Hinn
& William Matt McDowell

B♭(G)
F/A(D/F♯)
Gm(Em)
F(D)
1.
D.C. (v.2)
E♭(C)
I give my-self a-way, so you can use me. Take my
2.
E♭(C)
F(D)
D.S.
3.
E♭(C)
Tag
B♭(G)
use me. I give my-self a-way, use me. My life is not my own, to
F/A(D/F♯)
Gm(Em)
F(D)
1.-3.
E♭(C)
you I be-long; I give my-self, I give my-self to you. My
4.
E♭(C)

Here I'm standing with the rain on my face

(Where the mercy falls)

Key = D

David Ruis & Bob Hartry

♩ = 75

Bm7
G
faith to be-lieve; I'm wait-ing here, stand-ing where the mer-cy falls.
faith to be-lieve; we're wait-ing here, stand-ing where the mer-cy falls.
D(add4)
Chorus
A
A7
Streng-then fee-ble hands and
Bm7
A
stea-dy the knees, say-ing to the fear-ful heart
A7
Gmaj7
(Small notes 2nd time)
1.,2.
D(add4)
our God is com-ing, our God is here.
G D(add4)
1st time D.C. (v.2)
2nd time D.S.
3.
Bm7

A
G
Mid section
You are here,
Bm7
A
G
breaking through,
meeting us.
aah,
aah,
Bm7
A
Gmaj7
Aah,
aah,
D.C.(v.1) al Coda
N.C.
G D(add4)
G D(add4)
Coda
Bm7
G
I'm waiting here,
standing where the mercy falls.
D(add4)
G D(add4)

elevation kids
because kids deserve the best
www.elevationmusic.com/elevationkids
Spring Harvest
the big start 2
A collection of favourite worship songs from the Big Start
Spring Harvest introduces the Big Start CD, a brand new resource for all-age worship, starting your day with life and colour.
Brand new CD
DISCOVER MORE FROM ELEVATION KIDS HERE
Available from EssentialChristian.com or your local Christian bookstore
essential christian

24

Hope fills my soul

(Glorious)

Key = E

Bryan & Katie Torwalt

A(G)
C♯m(Bm)
shown brings re - fresh - ing like the
hold, for you have bro - ken the
B(A)
E(D)
rain; and peace floods my
chains, and now joy fills my
C♯m(Bm)
A(G)
heart, I've known no - thing a - part,
life, your Spi - rit, your light;
C♯m(Bm)
B(A)
Chorus
a - part from your good - ness, God. 1. You are
I'm un - done by the kind - ness of Christ.

C♯m(Bm) B/D♯(A/C♯) E(D) A(G) C♯m(Bm)
glo - ri - ous, and you are ho - ly, ho -
soul cries out that you are ho - ly, ho -
(2°)
B(A) C♯m(Bm) B/D♯(A/C♯) E(D) A(G)
ly; the hea - vens shout, that you are wor -
ly; the na - tions will shout, that you are wor -
1.,4. D.C. (al fine) 2.,3. D.S. (ch.2)
C♯m(Bm) B(A) B(A)
- thy, wor - thy. Whoah, - thy. 2. And my
- thy, wor -
B(A) A(G) C♯m(Bm)
- thy, oh, oh.
E(D) 1. B(A) 2. B(A)
And at the

THIS SONG WAS ONE OF THE REASONS
WE HAD SUCH A GREAT TIME RECORDING
"THE SOURCE: NEW SONGS FOR THE CHURCH"

25 How can it be, the One who died

(Christ is risen, he is risen indeed)

Key = A

Keith Getty,
Kristyn Getty & Ed Cash

♩. = 60

Last time to Coda
A E F♯m7 Bm7 A/C♯
lu - jah!" Join the cho-rus, sing with the re-deemed: Christ is ri-sen, he's
D.S. (last chorus repeat) al Coda
Esus4 A5
D.C.
ri - sen in - deed
3. Where
5. The
Coda
Esus4 A5
Tag
A/C♯
ri-sen in - deed He's a-live, he's a-live,
D2 A/E D2
hea - ven's gates are o - pened wide. He's a-live,
A/C♯ D2
1.
A/E D2
he's a-live now in hea - ven glo - ri-fied. He's a-

IN THE PRESENCE OF THE SON

You are the Son of God,
we have forgiveness in your presence.
You are the source of our salvation,
we have eternity in your presence.
You are the source of all hope,
we have comfort in your presence.
You are the source of all truth,
we have freedom in your presence.

I feel the heat is rising

(Fire never sleeps)

Key = F♯m

Martin Smith
& Nick Herbert

(v.2)
(v.3)
D
A
1.
Bm
scat-tered on the floor.
where your fire ne-ver sleeps.
and see a fire that ne-ver sleeps.
This fi-re ne-ver sleeps,
F♯m
D
A
Bm
D.C. (v.2)
his fi-re ne - ver sleeps.
3.
Bm
F♯m
E
Your fi-re ne-ver sleeps,
your fi-re ne - ver sleeps.
D
Jump to 𝄋
2.
A
E/G♯

Chorus
F♯m D A
Burn, oh my soul,
Bm F♯m D
set me on fi - re. Burn, oh my
A Bm F♯m
soul, light up the fi - re. Burn,
Last time to Coda
D A
oh my soul.
1. Bm D.C.(v.3)
2. Bm F♯m D
This fi-re ne-ver sleeps, his fi-re ne - ver sleeps.

Mid section
A Bm F♯m D
Pu - ri - fy my
A F♯m D
heart, pu - ri - fy my
A G♯m
heart. Spi - rit
E B
fall on us, Spi - rit fall on
2nd time D.S. al Coda
4 times F♯m D A Bm
(us.)

HE will not let your foot slip....

he who watches over you will

NOT

slumber

PSALM 121:3

27 I have tasted of your favour

(Holding on)

Key = F♯m

Simon Brading
& Anna Brading

1.
D.C. (v.2)
F♯m
D
me.
2. I've stared
2.,3.
Mid section
A
E
A
D
me. Shall we see you in the bless - ings, yet for -
(Tacet 1st time)
E
F♯m
D
E
A/C♯
get you in the trials? No, in all of these things you are
D
A
Bm
3
D
D.S. (2nd time al Coda)
work - ing, so I'll stand and trust you now. You're
Coda
D
E
D
E
F♯m
D
hold - ing on you're hold - ing on

28

I was lost, you took me in

(Where would I be?)

Key = B♭

Capo 3 (G)

Patrick Ryan Clark
& Jason Ingram

B♭(G) F(D) B♭/D(G/B) E♭(C) B♭(G) F/A(D/F♯)
un-end - ing mer - cy? I have life be-cause his life was laid down; I
(D.S. for last chorus repeat al Coda)
Last time to Coda
1.
D.C. (v.2)
E♭(C) F(D) Gm(Em)
won't look back now.
2.
E♭2(C2) Gm(Em) E♭(C) B♭(G) F(D)
Gm(Em) E♭(C) B♭(G) Dm(Bm)
Mid section
B♭(G) E♭(C)
His right - eous - ness is my
B♭(G) F(D) Cm(Am) E♭(C)
right - eous - ness in him, I will rest.

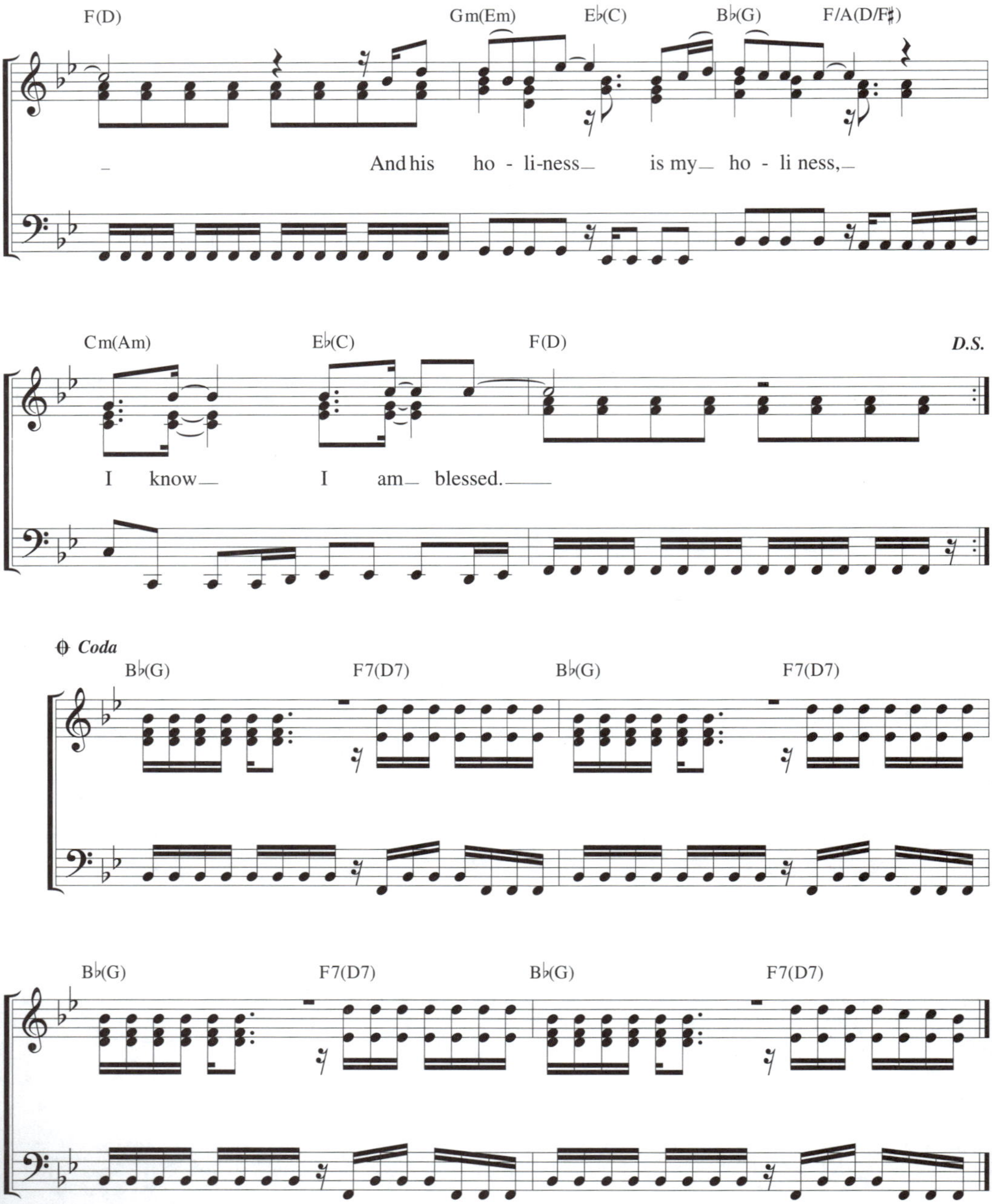
F(D)
Gm(Em)
E♭(C)
B♭(G)
F/A(D/F♯)
And his ho - li-ness is my ho - li ness,
Cm(Am)
E♭(C)
F(D)
D.S.
I know I am blessed.
Coda
B♭(G)
F7(D7)
B♭(G)
F7(D7)
B♭(G)
F7(D7)
B♭(G)
F7(D7)

I worship you Almighty God

(Nothing without you)

Capo 2 (D)
Key = E
♩ = 70
Kristian Ponsford
Verse
R.H.
E(D)
F♯m7+4(Em7+4)
Asus2(Gsus2)
Bsus4(Asus4)
3
I wor - ship you Al - migh - ty God, for your
hand is al - ways lead - ing me, each step I take
draws me clos - er, oh, so close
now, that all I see is you. And
ev - 'ry - thing beau - ti - ful'y fades a - way, and I

F♯m7+4(Em7+4)
Badd4(Aadd4)
Chorus
stand and sim - ply sing your name. And Lord, as your pre -
A(G) B(A) E(D) A(G) B(A)
- sence fills this place, may your glo - ry be found in our
E(D) A(G) B(A) C♯m7(Bm7)
praise. 'Cause all I have and e - ver will be, is no - thing with - out
F♯m7(Em7) Bsus4(Asus4) A(G) B(A)
you, no - thing with - out you. So let the walls shake with the cry of your
E(D) A(G) B(A) E(D)
name, let my life re - sound with the claim that you are my King,

A(G) B(A) C♯m7(Bm7) F♯m7(Em7) A(G)
my Sa - viour, my Lord. Ho - ly One, my friend, on bend - ed knee a -
Bsus4(Asus4)
1.
E(D)
D.C.
dored: I wor - ship you. I wor - ship
2.
E(D)
you.

30 If faith can move the mountains

(Waiting here for you)

Key = C

♩ = 64

Chris Tomlin, Martin Smith
& Jesse Reeves

Am Gsus4
2.,3.
C
2. You're the Lord with our hands
Dm7 Am G7sus4 F2 F F2
lift - ed high in praise, and it's you
Last time to Coda
C Dm7 Am7 G7sus4
we a - dore, sing - ing al - le -
1.
Am7 G7sus4 C
lu - ia.
D.C.(v.3)
Am Gsus4 C Am Gsus4
3. You are ev -

We like this song so much that we recorded it and put it on "The Source: New Songs for the Church"!

If I have you and nothing else

(Center of it all)

31

Key = G

♩ = 127

Jon Egan, Matt Redman,
Ben Fielding & Jason Ingram

1.
D.C. (v.2)
2.
Chorus
D
G
of you.
2. I'm los - ing my
You are the cen -
C
G
Em7
- ter of it all, You are the Sa - viour of my soul.
of great - est price; Je - sus, a - lone be lift - ed high.
Last time to Coda
D
C
Em7
You are the source of life, How could I not cry, Lord?
You are the source of life, you're the cen - ter of it all.
1.,3.
2.
D.C.(v.3)
4.
D
You are the hope
3. You are the
Mid section
C
D
Em
G
My heart thirsts for you a - lone, my heart thirsts for you a - lone,

C D Em G
my heart thirsts for you a - lone.
C D Em G
My eyes look to you and on - ly you. My soul longs for you and on - ly you.
D.S. (inc. rpt) al Coda
C D Em G
My heart thirsts for you a - lone. You are the cen -
Coda
D C Em7 D
You are the source of life; you're the cen - ter of it all.
C Em7 D
You are the source of life; you're the cen - ter of it all.

32 In my weakness I will come

(Draw me close)

Key = F

Nikki Fletcher, Luke Hellebronth
& Joel Wardle

Capo 3 (D)

Gm(Em) F/B♭(D/G) B♭(G) Dm7(Bm7) C(A)
close, I am lost with - out you; help me know I am yours
close, I will walk be - side you; this I know God is here
B♭(G) F/B♭(D/G) B♭(G) F/B♭(D/G)
1.,3.
2. D.S. (v.2)
B♭(G)
a - lone.
with me.
4.
B♭sus2(Gsus2) B♭(G) F(D) C(A) Gm(Em) B♭(G) F(D) C(A)
Tag
F(D) B♭(G) Dm7(Bm7)
1.-3., 5.-7.
B♭(G)
You are with me al - ways, e - ven now you are here.
4.
B♭/C(G/A)
8.
B♭(G)
PHOTOCOPY THIS LEGALLY
WITH AN MRL LICENCE
FROM CCLI.CO.UK

33 In the midst of the darkness

(Exalted One)

Key = E

Capo 4 (C)

♩ = 86

Chris Brown, London Gatch,
Mack Brock & Wade Joye

2.,3.
A2(F2)
Chorus
A2(F2) E(C) Bsus4(Gsus4) C♯m7(Am7)
— you. — We lift our eyes to you, where our help — comes from; –
A2(F2) E(C) Bsus4(Gsus4) A2(F2) E(C)
– our hope is found in you. Je - sus, Lord of — all, — we lift our eyes to you;
Bsus4(Gsus4) C♯m7(Am7) A2(F2) E(C) Bsus4(Gsus4)
3rd time D.S.
(Omit 3rd time)
ex - alt - ed One, — ex - alted One. —
1st time D.C. (v.1.)
4th time D.C. v.3 al Coda
Mid section
A2(F2) E(C) Bsus4(Gsus4) A2(F2)
Your pro - mise stands, —
C♯m7(Am7) E(C)
your love en - dures, — no - thing can shake us stand -

LOVE IS MADE COMPLETE

(based on 1 John 4:12)

In believing the Word in Jesus Christ,
Love is made complete among us.
In living our lives for Jesus Christ,
Love is made complete among us.
In being baptised in Jesus Christ,
Love is made complete among us.
In rising to new life in Jesus Christ.
Love is made complete among us.

because kids deserve the best
elevation kids
BUMPER DIGI-SONGBOOK
Includes over 160 printable music scores with full thematic and Scripture indexes
Fantastic all-age worship resources
Pre-School Praise
Pre-School Praise Box Set 1: 36 Songs plus backing tracks
Pre-School Praise Box Set 2: 33 Songs plus backing tracks
Kids Praise Party
Kids Praise Party Box Set 1: 48 Tracks
Kids Praise Party Box Set 2: 46 Tracks
Spring Harvest
THE WORSHIP YEARS DIGITAL SONGBOOK 2006 → 2010
DIGITAL SONGBOOK FEATURING OVER 450 SONGS FROM THE SPRING HARVEST PRAISE 2006-2010 SONGBOOKS
Powered by PowerMusiclite
MUSIC MANAGEMENT SOFTWARE
- Transpose chord sheets instantly
- Add capo chords in any key; show fret number
- Mac users can access the chords and scores as PDFs
Available from EssentialChristian.com or your local Christian bookstore
essential christian

34

In this moment here I am

(God is coming)

Key = A

Tim Hughes
& Martin Smith

♩ = 136

D A C♯sus4
so I will wait for you.
can take what's wrong and make it right.
C♯
Bridge
D A
For my God is com-ing; we can hear
F♯m7 E D
the hea - vens roar. Hold on, get rea-dy for the
F♯m E
Chorus
A
glo-ry of the Lord. Here you come, to
D/A A D/A
run - ning to find me. King of the u - ni - verse,
light up the dark - ness, for - e - ver glo - ri - ous,

Last time to Coda
1.,3.,5.
Bm7
A
E
yes, our God is the God who saves.
yes, our God is the God who saves.
Here you come,
2.
D.C.(v.2)
4.
2. In our world
Here you come,
D/F♯
D
D/A
Mid section
F♯m
Great is the Lord,
you are Lord;

1.
2.
D.S. (inc. rpt) al Coda
F♯m/A F♯m
E6
E6
God is great.
Here you come,
Coda
E
D
E F♯m Bm7
E F♯m Bm7
Bm7 F♯m/A F♯m

35

In times of waiting

(Here is Jesus)

Key = D

Lara Martin
& Noel Robinson

♩ = 72

Bridge
A F♯7/A♯ Bm Bm/A
I know in who I trust, he is my God, and he ne-ver dis - ap-points.
G
Chorus
D E/D
Here is Je - sus, it's all a-bout to change; here is Je -
Last time to Coda
G/D Asus4 D
- sus, it's re-sur-rec - tion day. Here is Je - sus, he's
E/D G Bm
1.
C
call-ing out my name; the King of hope is here, the King
G Bm Asus4 A
D.C.(v.3)
2.
C
of hope is here. 3.When some-thing's He

Mid section
Em7
D/F♯
G
speaks the Word, his will is done; he is the Word, life
A
Em7
Bm
has come. He speaks the Word, his will is done, he
G
Asus4
A
D.S.
is the Word, life has come. Here is Je -
Coda
E/D
G/D
Asus4
A
call - ing out your name; here is Je - sus.
D
E7/D
G/D
A7sus4
A7
D

In your presence there is fullness of life
(God is here)

36

Key = A

Lara Martin

D
E
(All suf - fi - cient One.)
let the sick say I am well.
A
D
God is here,
let the weak say I am strong.
A
F♯m7
(Let the weak say I am strong.)
God is here,
his
1.
D.C. (v.2)
2.
D.S.
E
D
E
Chorus
won-ders to per-form.
God is here
3.
D
Tag
E
Oh, his wonders,
yes, his won - ders,
his

THE LIGHT OF CHRIST

From the darkness of the outside world
we have come into the light of Christ.
From the darkness of our own guilt
we have come into the light of Christ.
From the darkness of our own lack of faith
we have come into the light of Christ.
From the darkness of our own burdens
We have come into the light of Christ.

37 It's always like springtime with you

(This is what you do)

Key = Am

Matt Stinton
& Jeremy Riddle

♩ = 146

Fmaj7
Gsus4
G
D.C.
2. Mid section
C/E
(8va on repeat)
It's al - ways like
This is what you do,
F
G
this is what you do:
you make
me come a - live.
C/E
F
G
This is what you do,
this is what you do:
you make
(8va on repeat)
F
1.,2.,3.
G
me come a - live.
You make
me come a live.
You make
me come a - live.
4. Last time to Coda
G
Dm7

C/E
Fmaj7
G
1.
2. D.S. al Coda
Coda
Tag
C/E
F2
It's like I'm liv - ing for the first time, it's like I'm
Gsus4
1.-3.
G
4.
G
liv - ing for the first time. It's like I'm

I've got a river of living water

(Deep cries out)

38

Key = G

♩ = 150

William Mathews,
Amanda Gilbertson & Christiann Koepke

C
dance / jump in the ri - ver, dance / jump in the
1. ri - ver. 'Cause we're
2. ri - ver.
Mid section
G
Deep cries out, deep cries out to deep.
Am7
Deep cries out, deep cries out to deep. So
G/B
we cry out, we cry out to, you
Last time to Coda
C
Je - sus.
1. D.C.
2.,4. D.S. (al Coda)
3.
G
We're fall - ing in - to
walk - ing in - to
Am7
deep - er
deep - er

1.
2.
1.,2.
3.
C2
G/B
C
G
Tag
(Last time)
Coda
D.S.S.
D.S.
wa - ters, call - ing out to you. We're
wa - ters, go - ing af - ter
you.
If he goes to the left, then we'll
go to the left, and if he goes to the right then we'll go to the right. We're gon - na
jump, jump, jump, jump
dance, dance, dance, dance
shout, shout, shout, shout
in the ri - ver,
ev' - ry - bo - dy. If he
yeah!
you Je - sus.

39 Jesus we come to your table

(Jesus my victory (Communion song))

Key = G

Travis Ryan,
Brandon Collins & Brenton Brown

Last time to Coda
(no rpt 1st time)
C5
E5
D
liv - ing stream, the bread of life.
Lamb of God, my vic - to - ry.
G bass
Mid section (3rd time instrumental)
G
King of kings you laid your bo - dy down,
King of kings for - sa - ken for my sin,
(Small note 2nd time)
C
oh, what love that lets the lost be found.
Lamb of God and yet the Li - on wins.
Oh, what sa - cri -
Lift - ed high for
1.,3.
2nd time D.S. al Coda
Em
D
fice gi - ven for my gain,
all the world to see,
all who die in you will rise a - gain.
2.
(Instrumental)
Em
D
Je - sus my vic - to - ry.
Coda
Em
D/F♯
G
vic - to - ry.

40 Jesus you are our everything
(Hallelujah)

Key = F

Capo 3 (D)

Cath Woolridge

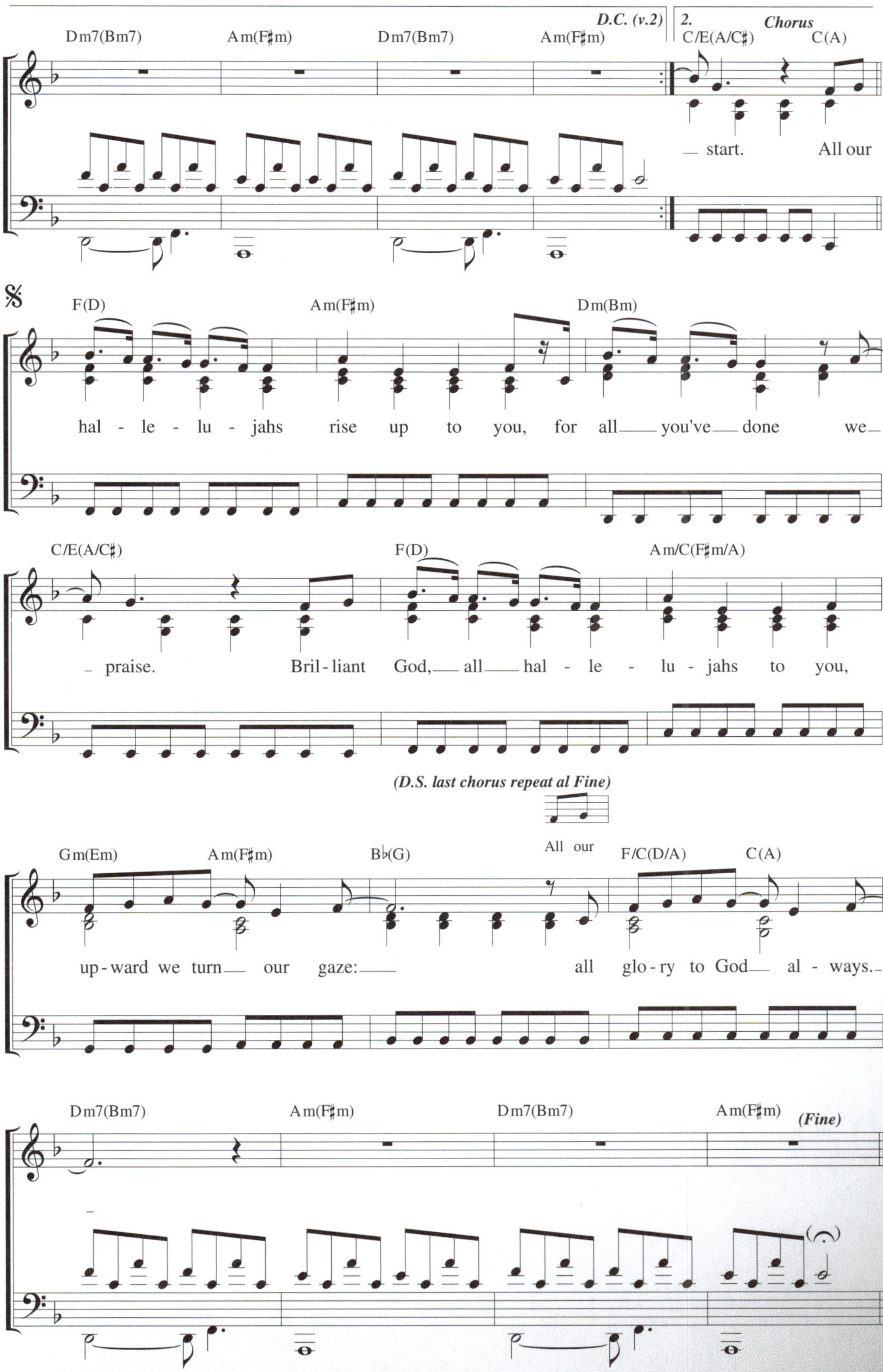
D.C. (v.2)
2.
Chorus
Dm7(Bm7) Am(F♯m) Dm7(Bm7) Am(F♯m) C/E(A/C♯) C(A)
start. All our
F(D) Am(F♯m) Dm(Bm)
hal - le - lu - jahs rise up to you, for all you've done we
C/E(A/C♯) F(D) Am/C(F♯m/A)
praise. Bril - liant God, all hal - le - lu - jahs to you,
(D.S. last chorus repeat al Fine)
All our
Gm(Em) Am(F♯m) B♭(G) F/C(D/A) C(A)
up - ward we turn our gaze: all glo - ry to God al - ways.
Dm7(Bm7) Am(F♯m) Dm7(Bm7) Am(F♯m)
(Fine)

Mid section
F(D)
B♭/F(G/D)
F(D)
C(A)
Dm(Bm)
Hal - le - lu - jah,
hal - le - lu - jah,
hal - le - lu - jah,
B♭(G)
F/C(D/A)
1.,2
C(A)
Dm(Bm)
B♭(G)
hal - le - lu - jah.
Hal - le - lu - jah,
3.
D.S.
C(A)
All our

King of love and grace

(Guardian)

Key = F

Capo 3 (D)

♩ = 105

Ben Cantelon, Nick Herbert
& Stu Garrard

Dm(Bm)
F/C(D/A)
C(A)
and if I wan - der, Love will find me. Good-ness and
B♭(G)
Am/C(F♯m/A) Dm(Bm)
mer - cy will al - ways fol - low. You go be -
F/C(D/A)
C(A)
F(D)
Last time to Coda
1st time D.C. (v.2)
fore me, my Guar - di - an.
Mid section
F(D)
You are God, our great de - fen - der, strong in love, for -
e - ver faith - ful. We are yours and we will trust in you.

FROM START TO FINISH

May the Gospels teach us the good news of Jesus, from start to finish.
May we live out the example of Jesus Christ, from start to finish.
May we never cease to encounter Jesus in our lives, from start to finish.
May time never distance us from our Saviour Jesus Christ, from start to finish.
And may we know – the Alpha and Omega – the one true Jesus Christ
in the race from start to finish.

42 Lift up, lift up your eyes

(The Kingdom is coming)

Key = C

♩ = 140

Sam Blake, Stephen Gibson,
Joel Pridmore & Ian Yates

Em
Am
– sing, our God reigns for - e -
Last time to Coda
1.
D.C.
2.
Dm2
F
ver, our God reigns. Lift reigns for - e -
F2
Mid section
G/B
Am
ver, The King-dom is com - ing,
G/B
C2
1.
G
(2°)
(the) hea-ven's draw - ing near.
2.
G
F
King of kings is here. The King-dom is com -

G Am G/B
- ing, The King-dom is com - ing, the King-dom is com - ing, the King-dom is com -
C
1.
G
(2°)
ing, (the) hea-ven's draw - ing near.
2.
D.S. al Coda
G
King of kings is here.
Coda
Dm2 F G Am
reigns. Oh,
(Fine)
G/B C G
oh, oh.

WORSHIP & REVIVAL

In conversation with Cath Woolridge from the 'Sound of Wales', Spring Harvest explores their vision.

'*Dyma gariad fel y moroedd*' - translated 'Here is love vast as the ocean' - became the love song of the 1904 Welsh Revival. Annie Davies, one of the famous characters of the revival, would often sing this outside pubs and witness the hardest of men, often coalminers and ocassionally drunk, become silent, deeply impacted and be led to the Lord. Crime rate dropped, drunkards reformed, pubs reported trade losses and even "football and rugby became uninteresting in the light of new joy and direction received by the converts".

108 years later, singers from the collaborative of musicians known as 'Sound of Wales' (SOW) gather in Cardiff city centre to sing acapella versions of revival hymns, festive tunes and self-penned songs to Christmas shoppers. Similar stirrings occur. Cath Woolridge explains how "crowds of people gathered round, some in tears, others asking for prayer or commenting on the different sound with a few inviting us to sing at their business functions over Christmas". The cultural and economic landscape may be different now than in Annie Davies' time, but this land of song is still responding to the rhythm of God.

Llef (The Cry)

Last year, a group of friends from different locations in Wales started to collaborate with the aim of declaring the good news of the gospel with music as the hallmark. One of their main objectives is to 'capture and release the sound of Wales'. Woolridge explains, "Wales is known as the *land of song* and the *land of great revival.* God has been stirring up a people within Wales to run with the baton that is in our spiritual inheritance and share with the nations the heritage of this land. We believe God wants us to release the sound of Wales to do a new thing. We serve a God of the impossible who is able to take broken and empty hearts and set them to beat again.

Merging the old with the new is a significant feature of their album 'Llef'. The love song of the Welsh revival and the strikingly poignant '*Dros Gymru'n Gwlad* (For Wales our Land)' sits alongside original SOW anthems including 'What the world is waiting for' and 'Hallelujah'. These new century songs and arrangements contain the same revival heart cry for the grace of God to be poured out on parched and barren land, for the Holy Spirit to move and transform lives and communities and for Jesus to be seen as the hope of the nations.

Language

There is intentionality in SOW to write and record songs in their own Welsh language. Embedded within their native dialect is a power-house of rich history and deep experiences and even though nostalgia may play an important part, Woolridge describes how "so many of the great hymns were written in Welsh suggesting a spiritual inheritance lies within the language, unlocking identity and pointing to our destiny. We feel it's important for every tribe and tongue to worship in their own language."

The R Word

In conversation with SOW, you quickly lose count of the times they mention the word 'revival'. They are passionate to see communities transformed and resourced and often substitute the R word for another – Revolution - of which they speak with equal enthusiasm! "There are misconceptions that revival is merely about hyped-up big meetings and often, momentary. Although God does move at specific moments, we are longing for a revolution to happen in people's hearts, an internal reaction to the God who created them and for hearts to turn to the new life. A revolution in Wales is where the reality of a living Saviour breaks into brokenness and, as a nation, we turn back to God and reflect His glory."

The music of SOW does sound amazing and their album 'Llef' has already received stunning accolades. More importantly, they carry the same fire of the early Welsh revivalists and as they sing out their anthems of praise, they are also praying for torrents of grace and encounters of forgiveness to once again flow through the valleys, transforming lives and communities.

For more details of SOW visit **www.sowmusic.co.uk**

43

Light in my darkness

(All my hope)

Key = C

♩ = 80

Reuben Morgan
& Jason Ingram

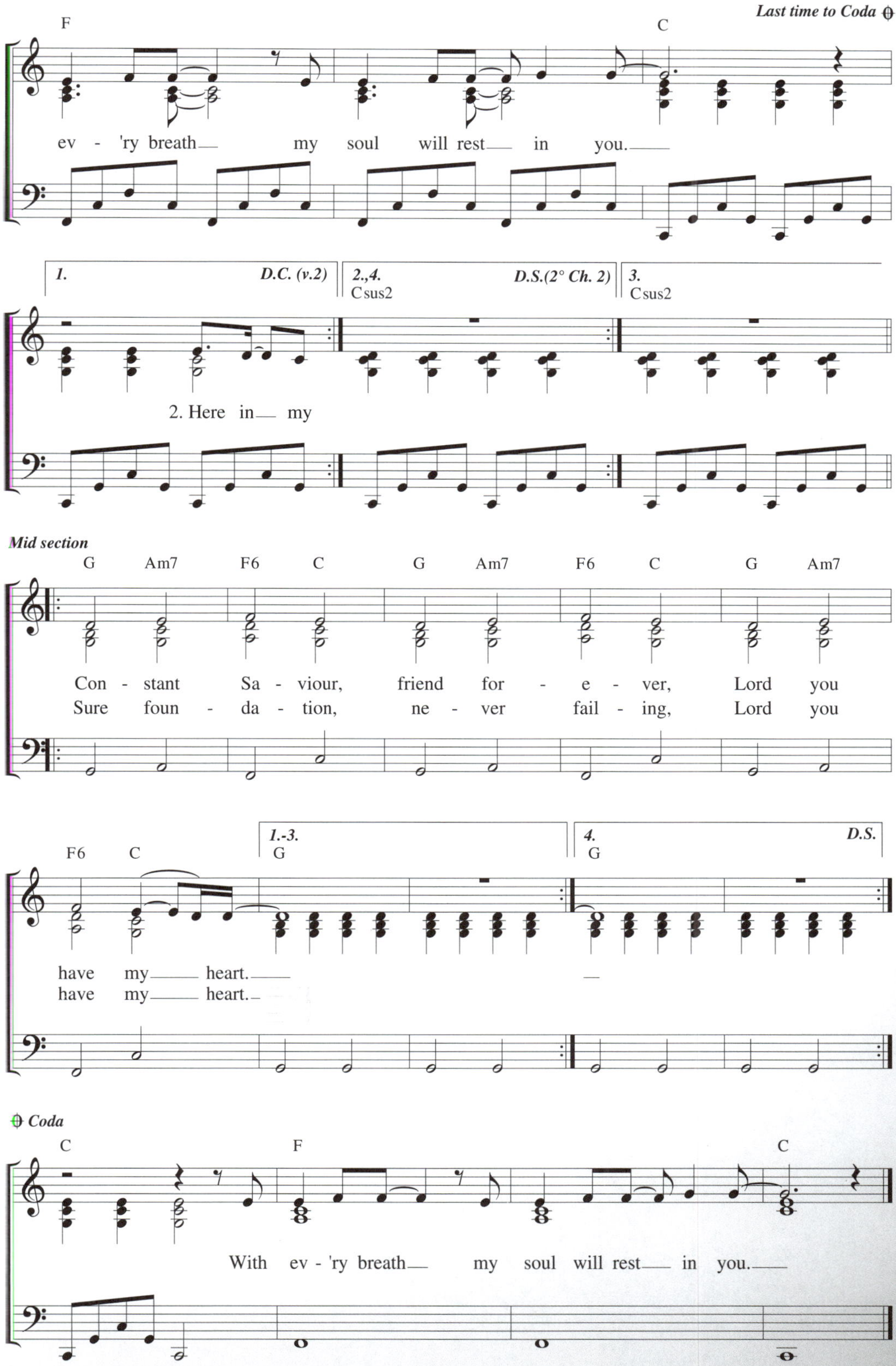
Last time to Coda
F C
ev - 'ry breath my soul will rest in you.
1. D.C. (v.2)
2.,4. D.S.(2° Ch. 2)
Csus2
3.
Csus2
2. Here in my
Mid section
G Am7 F6 C G Am7 F6 C G Am7
Con - stant Sa - viour, friend for - e - ver, Lord you
Sure foun - da - tion, ne - ver fail - ing, Lord you
1.-3.
4. D.S.
F6 C G G
have my heart.
have my heart.
Coda
C F C
With ev - 'ry breath my soul will rest in you.

44 Lord I desire to live as one

(Invade my heart)

Key = B♭

Capo 3 (G)

♩ = 104

Lyrics: Cath Woolridge
Music: Jon Goode & Cath Woolridge

B♭(G)
E♭maj7(Cmaj7)
1st time D.C. (v.2)
2. The
3. I
Verse
(v.4)
B♭(G)
E♭maj7(Cmaj7)
can - not let a - ny - thing hold me back from you.
you, O Lord, true liv - ing vine, my fa - mished soul to feast;
B♭(G)
I must press on in Christ, stand strong, in
I ban - quet on this love di - vine, my
E♭maj7(Cmaj7)
B♭(G)
faith must con - stant try. To stand, to choose to stand
praise to ne - ver cease. All glo - ry to God, I'm lift -

E♭maj7(Cmaj7)
in you, my - self stand out the way; it's
- ed in awe, to the things in Christ I see; I
B♭(G)
God o' - er all, you for - e - ver reign your
hate my sin, but love my Sa - viour:
E♭maj7(Cmaj7)
Chorus
E♭(C)
way I will o - bey.
3. We wor - ship you,
thank you for res - cu - ing me.
4. In - vade my heart,
Gm(Em)
F(D)
E♭(C)
wor - ship you, we wor - ship you,
in - vade my heart, in - vade my heart

Last time to Coda
2nd time D.S.S. al Coda
Gm(Em)
F(D)
B♭(G)
– wor - ship you, to - day.
– come stay. 4. In -
E♭maj7(Cmaj7)
D.S. (v.4)
4. In
Coda
Gm(Em)
F(D)
E♭(C)
– stay.
Gm(Em)
F(D)
E♭(C)

45

Lord teach me your ways

(What the world is waiting for)

Key = D♭

Capo 1 (C)

Lyrics: Cath Woolridge
Music: Jon Goode & Cath Woolridge

D♭/F(C/E)
G♭(F)
A♭sus4(Gsus4)
all you've done, your sa - cri - fice and mer - cy.
gave me grace, you took my place, it is fin - ished.
A♭(G)
1.
B♭m(Am)
G♭(F)
D♭/F(C/E)
D.C. (v.2)
2. Chorus
A♭(G)
G♭(F)
D♭(C)
You are what the world is wait - ing for;
E♭m(Dm)
B♭m(Am)
you are what the world is wait - ing for.
B♭m(Am)
G♭(F)
You are what the world is wait - ing for,

D♭/F(C/E)
A♭(G)
you are what the world is de - spe - rate for.
B♭m(Am)
G♭(F)
You are what the world is search - ing for, it's all in you,
2nd time D.S. (with repeats)
D♭/F(C/E)
A♭(G)
Christ Je - sus it's in you.
E♭m7(Dm7)
B♭m(Am)
A♭(G)
Christ Je - sus it's in you, on - ly you.
E♭m7(Dm7)
B♭m(Am)
A♭(G)
G♭(F)
Christ Je - sus it's in you, on - ly in you.

46

Love set me free

(Heaven)

Key = A

Pete James

♩ = 86

Verse
A
D
1. Love set me free; the
2. Love bec - kons me; the
3. I'll run with faith, I'll
Bm
A
E
God of hea - ven walked the earth for me.
tro - phies of this life won't mean a thing.
run with per - se - ve - rance through this race.
(vv.2,3)
A
D
Pur - chased by blood; my
Each day on earth com - plete, takes me
While hea - ven cheers my name, and yes, I
(v.3)
Bm
A
E
life has known the kiss of hea - ven's love.
clo - ser 'til we dance on gol - den streets for - e - ver.
know to live is Christ to die is gain, I'm sing - ing.

Great acoustic version of this one on "The Source: New Songs for the Church"

47 Love the Lord with all your heart

(God is love)

Key = A

♩ = 88

Nick Drake
& Becky Drake

JESUS IS ALL

Jesus, you are all, may you be all to us.
You are all love, may we be loving.
You are all hope, may we be hopeful.
You are all courage, may we be courageous.
You are all mercy, may we be merciful.
You are all passion, may we be passionate.
You are all vision, may we be visionary.
You are all, may you be all to us.

48

Mighty God

(God, you are stronger)

Key = D

Mark Tedder
& Jordan Riley

teach me
YOUR
way, Lord;

lead me in a
STRAIGHT PATH
because of my
oppressors

PSALM
27:11

49

My future hangs on this
(Second chance)

Key = D

♩= 72

Rend Collective Experiment

D Bm7 G D
3rd time D.S. (rpt chorus)
where my hope re-starts: a se-cond chance is hea - ven's heart.
1.
D.C. (v.2)
A D/F♯ G D A
2. When
2.,3.
Mid section
D A G
Count - less se - cond chan - ces we've been gi - ven at the
D A D A
cross. Count - less se - cond chan - ces we've been
i
D.C.(v.3)
ii
G D A D A D
gi - ven at the cross. 3. Frag cross.

50 My hope is built on nothing less

(Cornerstone)

Key = C

♩= 72

Jonas Myrin, Reuben Morgan & Eric Liljero
Verses from 'The Solid Rock' by Edward Mote (Trad.)

Have you heard the acoustic version of this song on "The Source: New Songs for the Church"?

51

Nothing can separate
(Your love never fails)

Key = A

Chris McClarney
& Anthony Skinner

♩ = 112

D A E D Chorus
You stay the same
A E/G♯ Bm A/C♯
through the a - ges; Your love ne - ver chang -
D A E/G♯
- es. There may be pain in the night, but joy comes with the morn -
Bm D A E/G♯
- ing. And when the o - ceans rage I don't have
Bm A/C♯ D A E/G♯
to be a-fraid be-cause I know that you love me and your

1.
D
F♯m
E
love ne - ver fails.
2.
D
Tag
F♯m
No vocal 1st time
All things work to - ge - ther for my
E
(Fine)
Repeat ad. lib. al fine
good.
You make

Nothing will change

(My hope)

52

Capo 3 (G)

♩ = 84

Key = B♭

Paul Baloche, Ed Kerr,
Sheila Rabe & Alyssa Mellinger

Chorus
E♭(C) Gm7(Em7) Fsus4(Dsus4) F(D) B♭(G)
I know you're al - ways good. My hope is built on
F(D) Gm7(Em7) E♭(C)
no-thing less than your great love, your right-eous-ness.
B♭(G) F(D) Gm7(Em7)
I will not walk a - no-ther way. I trust your heart, I
E♭(C) (Fine) F(D) Gm7(Em7) E♭(C)
trust your name. I'm hold-ing on, I'm
Fsus4(Dsus4) F(D) 1. E♭(C) B♭(G)
hold-ing on to you.

D.C.(v.3)
2.,3.
1st time D.S.
Fsus4(Dsus4)
F(D)
Gm7(Em7)
E♭(C)
E♭(C)
(2. Oh,)
Mid section
B♭(G)
F(D)
I'm hold-ing on, I'm hold - ing on to you.
Gm7(Em7)
E♭(C)
4th time D.S. al fine
I'm hold-ing on, I'm hold - ing on to you.

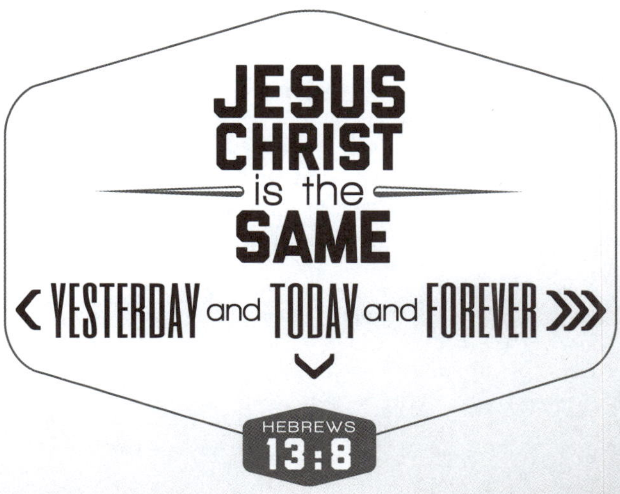
JESUS
CHRIST
is the
SAME
YESTERDAY and TODAY and FOREVER
HEBREWS
13:8

53 Oh God of power, living word

(Our song from age to age)

Key = G

Joel Sczebel

C Am Em C
pro - mised grace would come to save, to loose death's i - ron hold.
glad - ness we now bear your name, and wor - ship at your feet.
have no doubt you'll lead us home, to fi - n'ly see your face.
sing as all the heav'ns re - sound for all e - ter - ni - ty.
D Chorus G D
1. You are our song from age to age, our voi - ces u - nite to re -
2. You are our song from age to age, we will pro - claim your
(No repeat 1st time)
1.
D.C. (v.2)
C Em G
count your praise a - gain and a - gain.
pow'r to save a - gain and a - gain.
2. Oh
2.,3.,4.
Last time to Coda
D.C.(v.3.,4.)
G C
3. Oh
4. Oh

Coda
G

HEY - DID YOU KNOW?
IF YOU'RE PHOTOCOPYING THIS, YOU NEED AN MRL LICENCE FROM CCLI.CO.UK

54 Oh the deep, deep love of Jesus

Key = G

Words and music: Graham Kendrick
First stanza of chorus: Samuel Trevor Francis (1834-1925)

C G/B Am D G Em G 7/D
vast, un-mea-sured, bound - less, free. Deep - er than the deep - est o-cean
1.
C G/B Am D G Em C G/B
is my Sa-viour's love for me.
D.C.(v.3)
2.
Mid section
Em D/F♯ Am D G Cm/E♭
love for me. Though it seems at
G/B Cm Am D G
times he's sleep - ing while the tow - 'ring wa - ters rage, ev - er-last - ing
Em Em/D C Am D G Em
arms sur-round me, al - ways, al - ways.

Dedicated to the the world's 1.2 million merchant seafarers and to the Sailors' Society.

This can work great with a small band! Hear an acoustic arrangement on "The Source: New Songs for the Church"

Only one name

55

Capo 2 (Em)

♩ = 130

Key = F♯m

Pete James

Verse
F♯m(Em)
D(C)
1. On - ly one name, strong e - nough to save;
one name spans the breadth of time,
(v.2)
E(D)
F♯m(Em)
D(C)
on - ly one name, o - ver - comes the grave.
on - ly one name, hu - man and di - vine.
(v.2)
E(D)
Bm(Am)
D(C)
On - ly one name, is the hope of all the earth;
On - ly one name, to whom ev - 'ry knee will bow:
E(D)
D(C)
E(D)
ri - sen Sa - viour, he is Je - sus.
King of Hea - ven, he is Je - sus.

Chorus
A(G) D(C) Bm7(Am)
So we sing it through the streets and shout it from the roof tops:
E(D) A(G) D(C) Bm7(Am)
Je - sus saves! He's a-live, he's a - live and we be - lieve that
Last time to Coda
(D.S. for last chorus repeat)
E(D) D(C) E(D) A(G)
Je - sus saves, Je - sus saves!
1. D.C. (v.2) 2.
Mid section
D(C)
2. On - ly He is the an - swer for this
E(D) A(G) E/G♯(D/F♯) F♯m(Em)
world, he is the an - swer for the soul al -

D(C)
E(D)
ways, al - ways.
1.
2.
D.S al Coda
He is the
Coda
E(D)
D(C)
E(D)
Je - sus saves!
Je - sus saves!
A(G)
Je - sus saves!

56 Outside the city walls

(Love so high)

Key = D

Reuben Morgan, Chris Tomlin,
Jason Ingram & Matt Redman

♩ = 70

G Bm7 A Asus4 A D D/C♯
love, deep - er than the sea. Your love so sure,
Bm7 D/A G Bm7
stron - ger than the moun - tains, oh, your love, it's ev - 'ry - thing to me.
2nd time D.S. for chorus repeat
A Asus4 A
1.
G A G/B A/C♯
how deep, how wide, how long, how high.
(Your)
D G2 D G2
D.C. (v.2)
2.
G A G/B A/C♯
Play 3 times
deep, how wide, how long, how high. (How)

Take a listen to this song on "The Source: New Songs for the Church"

PRE-ORDER NOW
AVAILABLE JULY 2013
Spring Harvest
Spring Harvest
2013
Bottled At
THE SOURCE
LIVE WORSHIP FROM
SPRING HARVEST
LEAD WORSHIPPERS
MARK BESWICK * PETE JAMES * LARA MARTIN * CHRIS McCLARNEY * NOEL ROBINSON
LIVE WORSHIP FROM
SPRING HARVEST 2013
Spirit-soaked live worship from
Spring Harvest's Big Top
LEAD WORSHIPPERS
MARK BESWICK
PETE JAMES
LARA MARTIN
CHRIS McCLARNEY
NOEL ROBINSON
Available from EssentialChristian.com
or your local Christian bookstore
essential christian

57 Place my head on a rock

(Jacob)

Key = B

Capo 4(G)

Tim O'Hare
& Andy Smith

1.
D.C.
G♯m(Em) E(C) B(G) F♯(D) G♯m(Em) E(C) B(G) F♯(D)
Place my
2. Mid section
G♯m(Em) E(C) B(G) F♯(D) G♯m(Em) E(C)
This is the gate of hea - ven, this is the house of God;
This is the gate of hea - ven, this is the house of God;
B(G) F♯(D) G♯m(Em) E(C) B(G) F♯(D)
o - pen the gate of hea - ven to us.
pour out the oil of hea - ven on us.
1.
G♯m(Em) E(C) B(G) F♯(D)
2.
D.S. al Coda
G♯m(Em) E(C) B(G) F♯(D)
Sing - ing
Coda
(repeat ad-lib to finish)
G♯m(Em) E(C) B(G) F♯(D) G♯m(Em)

58

Praise you in the morning

(Praise you)

Key = G

Andy Smith

Gsus2 G Gsus4 G Gsus4
praise you in the eve - ning when I'm lay - ing down my crowns, and I'm
Bridge
G Gsus2 G Gsus2 G
sa - tis - fied in you and you a - lone. You are my por -
Am Em G
- tion, my strong De - liv - 'rer, migh - ty in pow - er, un - end - ing in love.
D7 Am Em
You are ex - al - ted, in ev - 'ry sea - son; be - cause of your good -
Chorus
C D Dsus4 G
- ness, Lord, we come. 1. We will sing our prais - es,
(2.) fi - nal day when I've

G/B C
voic - es raised, and to - ge - ther let our 'hal - le - lu - jahs' rise; in ev - 'ry sea -
run this race and I'm stand - ing in the beau - ty of your light; in ev - 'ry sea -
(4th time)
1st time D.C.
4th time D.S.
Last time to Coda
- son.
(And we will)
Am D G Gsus2 G
- son for - e - ver you are glo - ri - fied.
1. D.S.
2.
Gsus4 G Gsus2 G
Gsus4 G Gsus2 G C
2. And on that
Gm/B♭ A 7
Cm6/E♭
D.S (with repeat) al Coda
And we will

Coda
G Gsus2 G Gsus4 G A7
Oh, in ev-'ry sea - son, for -
D C
e - ver you are glo - ri - fied.
Gm/B♭ A7
Cm/E♭ Cm6/E♭
Tag
C
Ev-'ry morn-ing
we will praise you.
Gm/B♭ A7
and in ev-'ry eve-'ning we praise you, in ev-'ry

If you have a smaller worship group,
the acoustic version of this song on
"The Source: New Songs for the Church"
might give you some arrangement ideas...

59

Resting in your promise

(Defender)

Key = B♭

Capo 3 (G)

♩ = 70

Chris McClarney, John Hartley, Miriam Webster,
Michael Tyler, Case Crayenord & Henk Pool

Cm7(Am7) Bridge B♭(G) F(D) Cm7(Am7) B♭(G)
And when I don't know what to do, Je - sus, I will fix my eyes on
F(D) Chorus B♭(G) Cm7(Am7)
you. You're my de-fen - der, I hide my hope in you, you are the lov-
Gm7(Em7) F(D) E♭maj7(Cmaj7)
- ing arms my bro - ken heart can run to. And I will re-mem-
Last time to Coda
B♭(G) Cm7(Am7)
- ber that there is no - thing you can't do, 'cause you are God,
1.,3.
2° D.S.S. al Coda
Gm7(Em7) F(D) E♭maj7(Cmaj7)
and you are good, and I sur-ren - der: you're my de-fen-

B♭(G)
E♭maj7(Cmaj7)
Gm7(Em7)
- der,
you're my de-fen - der.
D.C.(v.2)
2.
E♭maj7(Cmaj7)
B♭(G)
Mid section
2. You are
- der, oh.
A migh-ty for -
Cm7(Am7)
Gm7(Em7)
E♭(C)
- tress is our God,
I will not fear,
I will not fear.
B♭(G)
Cm7(Am7)
Gm7(Em7)
E♭maj7(Cmaj7)
D.S.
Safe and se-cure here in your will,
I will not fear.
Coda
Gm7(Em7)
F/A(D/F♯)
E♭maj7(Cmaj7)
and you are good,
and I sur-ren - der:

60 Seated above, enthroned in the Father's love

(Overcome)

Key = A

Jon Egan

2.
Chorus
A2
Sa - viour,
Je - sus,
F♯m7
wor - thy of ho - nour and glo - ry, wor - thy of all of our
awe - some in po - wer for - e - ver, awe - some and great is your
Last time to Coda
E
D2
A2
praise, you o - ver - came.
name, you o - ver - came.
1.
D.C.(v.3)
D2
2.
D2
A2
F♯m7
Mid section
E
D2
A2
F♯m7
We will o - ver - come by the blood of the Lamb and the

AS YOUR PEOPLE

We carry the name of Jesus – we are your people.
As your people we are called by you.
As your people we give the right example.
As your people we fight for the truth.
As your people we care for the rejected.
As your people we seek justice.
As your people we make a true difference.
As your people we carry the name of Jesus – we are your people.

LIVE AT
SPRING HARVEST
PETE JAMES
LIVE AT
SPRING HARVEST
FEATURING
ONLY ONE NAME, MY HEART IS SINGING LOUD & 10,000 REASONS
TRENT
LIVE AT
SPRING HARVEST
FEATURING PERFECT SACRIFICE,
UNFAILING LOVE, NOW AND EVER AND FRIEND OF GOD
TWO STIRRING
WORSHIP ALBUMS
RECORDED LIVE
IN THE
SPRING HARVEST BIG TOP
Available from EssentialChristian.com
or your local Christian bookstore
essential christian

61

Since the dawn of all creation

(Let this be the time)

Key = A♭

Capo 1 (G)

Pete James

♩ = 76

E♭sus4(D) E♭(D) E♭sus2(D) Chorus E♭(D)
_ in your church_ a - gain.___ 1. Let this be the time_
_ on the streets,_ hea - ven's love___
A♭(G)
_ for your King - dom to come,___ here on the earth_
(2.)_ for your Spi - rit to move,___ to wa - ken our hearts_
Last time to Coda
Fm7(Em) B♭m(Am)
_ for your will to be done;___ your love is a - maz - ing,___
_ with a pas - sion re - newed;___ your love is a - maz - ing,___
1. D.C. (v.2) 2. D.S. (ch.2)
B♭/A♭(A/G) G♭(F) E♭(D)
your love is a - maz - ing.___ 2. We're cry - ing out_

3.
B♭/A♭(A/G)
G♭(F)
E♭(D)
Mid section
your love is a - maz - ing.
Let
D♭(C)
E♭(D)
D♭(C)
love come and fill our hearts, lead us to the
A♭(G)
E♭/G(D/F♯)
D♭(C)
E♭(D)
world you love, let love come and fill our hearts.
G♭(F)
A♭(G)
Fm7(Em)
B♭m(Am)

There's a really great acoustic version of this song on "The Source: New Songs for the Church"

62 Sing, north to the south

(Sing starry heavens)

Key = B♭

Capo 3 (G)

♩ = 104

Graham Kendrick
& Noel Robinson

Chorus
B♭(G)
E♭/B♭(C/G)
F7(D7)
E♭(C)
Sing, star - ry hea - vens, sing, an - gel host a - dor - ing,
Last time to Coda
1.
D.C. (v.2)
F(D)
E♭/F(C/D)
sing, all you na - tions, wor - ship the King.
3.
D.S. al Coda
2.
Mid section
King.
King.
Shout it out, from the high-est hea-ven.
Sing it back, all God's peo - ple.
B♭sus4(Gsus4)
G♭(E♭)
Je - sus reigns a - bove
all: lift your voice and lead the an - them.
D.S.

Coda
F(D)
B♭(G)
E♭/F(C/D)
F7(D7)
King. Wor - ship the King of
B♭(G)
B♭sus4(Gsus4)
B♭(G)
kings.
B♭sus4(Gsus4)
B♭(G)
Rit.

The Kingdom of our God is near

(Our God is mercy)

Key = A

Capo 2(G)

♩ = 130

Brenton Brown,
Eoghan Heaslip & Nick Herbert

D(C)
heavy, if your soul is thirsty, there is a
F♯m7(Em7)
E(D)
refuge, a home for the lonely, 'cause our God is
A(G)
E(D)
F♯m(Em)
D(C)
near, our God is near, our God is
Last time to Coda
A(G)
E(D)
F♯m(Em)
D(C)
near, our God is near.
Mid section
A(G)
D/A(C)
Lift up your eyes, lift up your eyes, lift up your eyes and sing.

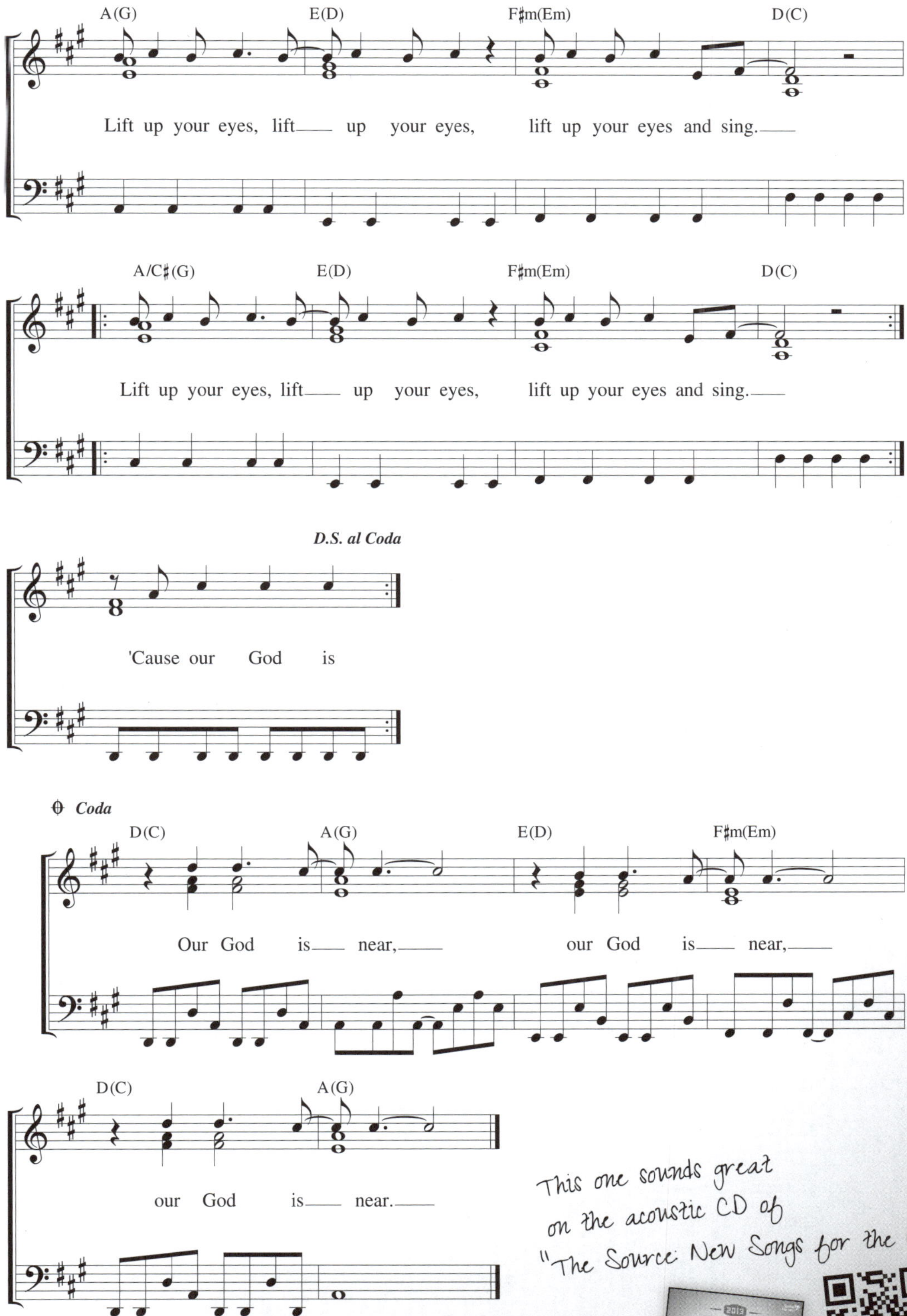

This one sounds great
on the acoustic CD of
"The Source: New Songs for the Church"

64 The Spirit of the Sovereign Lord

(From ashes to beauty)

Key = F

Capo 3 (D)

Tom Read

♩ = 74

Last time to Coda
F(D) Dm7(Bm7) B♭(G) C(A) F(D) Dm7(Bm7)
would you take these hands of mine and use me. Pour your Spi-rit o - ver me,
B♭(G) C(A) F(D) Dm7(Bm7)
let your love rain down; would you take these feet of mine
1.
B♭(G) C(A) F(D) C/E(A/C♯) Dm7(Bm7) C/E(A/C♯) F(D) C/E(A/C♯)
and lead me.
D.C. (v.2)
Dm7(Bm7) C/E(A/C♯)
2. The
3.
D.S. al Coda
B♭(G) C(A)
and use me.
2.
B♭(G) C(A) F(D)
and lead me.
Mid section
Am7(F♯m7) Dm7(Bm7) Gm7(Em7)
You lead me to the poor, That's where you are.

Have you heard the acoustic version of this song on "The Source: New Songs for the Church"?

The well is dry and I am weak

65

(Rain)

Capo 4 (G)

Key = B

♩ = 130

Mark Tedder
& Jordan Riley

Chorus
E(C)
G♯m7(Em7)
B(G)
You put a new song in our hearts, you are sing -
G♯m7(Em7)
C♯m7(Am7)
G♯m7(Em7)
- ing o - ver us, you put a new song in our hearts.
1.,3.,5.
F♯(D)
2.,4.,6.
F♯(D)
1st time D.C. (v.2)
3rd time to Coda
(We're sing - ing.)
(We're sing - ing.)
Mid section
B sus4(Gsus4)
B(G)
B sus2(Gsus2)
B(G)
Let our songs be to you for - e - ver,
Let our lives be to you for - e - ver,
B sus4(Gsus4)
B(G)
B sus2(Gsus2)
B(G)
let our love be to you for - e - ver.
let our praise be to you for - e - ver.

REACHING OUT PRAYER

(based on 1 John 4:7)

Dear friends, let us reach out beyond our boundaries and by breaking down barriers.

Let us love one another for love comes from God.

Dear friends, let us reach out to welcome the unloved and 'unlovable'.

Let us love one another for love comes from God.

Dear friends, let us reach out as Jesus did, by sharing love with others.

Let us love one another for love comes from God.

Let us reach out to all with the love of God.

66

The word of God is light in my darkness

(Word of God)

Key = A

Andi Rozier
& Brenton Brown

♩ = 116

Chorus
D A E F♯m D A E/A
1.,3.
2.
4.
D.C.
Je - sus, faith - ful word of God, the an - chor of my heart; you're ev - 'ry - thing you say you are. now.
Great - er than my deep - est needs, the ground be - neath my feet, your pro - mis - es won't fail me
now.

We were really excited to have the chance to record this song for "The Source: New Songs for the Church"!

There is a name I love to hear

(Giving in)

67

Capo 4 (G)

♩ = 80

Key = B

Mark Tedder,
Brad Nyght & Chad Carouthers

Chorus
B(G)
F♯(D)
heal - ing in your name, there's po - wer in your name, sal -
free - dom in your name, com - pas - sion in your name, for -
C♯m(Am)
Last time to Coda
1.,3.,5.
E(C)
F♯(D)
va - tion in the name of Je - sus. There's
give - ness in the name of Je -
2.
E(C)
G♯m(Em)
B(G)
F♯(D)
- sus.
E(C)
G♯m(Em)
B(G)
D.C. (v.2)
4.
E(C)
F♯(D)
- sus.
C♯(A)
G♯m(Em)
B(G)
F♯(D)

Tag
G♯m(Em)
F♯/A♯(D/F♯)
I'm giv-ing in,
I'm giv-ing in,
B(G)
1.
E(C)
2.
E(C)
D.S.
I'm giv-ing in to your name.
There's
Coda
E(C)
G♯m(Em)
B(G)
F♯/A♯(D/F♯)
- sus.
E(C)
G♯m(Em)
B(G)
E(C)

68 There is more than I can imagine

(Invaded by your love)

Key = Em

♩ = 76

Tom Read, Dan Wheeler,
Tim Hughes & Ben Cantelon

Em9 Em Em9 Em
posed by your good - ness, clothed by your grace, how you
C G
love me, oh, you love me. De - li - vered in - to free - dom,
Em9 Em Em9 Em
bought at a price: to be healed, to be whole, to be gi - ven new life, how you
Last time to Coda
1.
C Em C G D
love me, oh, you love me.
D.C. (v.2)
2. Mid section
Em C G D D Em Am7 G
Oh, I'm cap - ti - va - ted by your

D Em Am7 G D Em
love, O Lord. Oh, I'm
D.S. (instrumental bridge) al Coda
Am7 G D/F♯ Em Am7 G
cap - ti - va - ted by your love, O Lord.
Coda
Em C G D/F♯ Em C G D/F♯
Em

ALL AGE WORSHIP - PLAYING AT WORSHIP?

All-age worship is perhaps a bit like Marmite... you either love it or hate it. Well, I love it! It often gets a bad press, but I hope that with a bit of a re-think we can re-envision and inspire our churches by re-imagining it.

While researching for my dissertation (on all-age worship) at London School of Theology, I discovered this quote from the theologian Geoffrey Wainwright:

> *'Worship can be seen as the explicitly religious form of play.'*

This phrase has stuck with me, and the more I think about worship being the play of the Church, the more I think he's totally hit the nail on the head...

Play is an interesting phenomenon. Somewhere along the way we have made playing exclusive to children and something that is much too silly for us mature adults! I'd like to suggest, however, that when we're thinking about worship, particularly all-age worship, we have a lot to learn from the art of play.

So, what's playing all about?

Play can unite people from different cultures, backgrounds and linguistic ability. It doesn't require us to be able to read, write or have a wide vocabulary.

Play is exciting and compels others to join in! As children, we don't play because we have to, we play because we just can't help ourselves. It's completely spontaneous, freely chosen, structure-free and wonderfully all-over-the-place! Actually, for it to be the most fun, exploratory play should be just that - exploratory - without ulterior motive.

Children's play can be: happy, sad, loud, active, quiet, calm, creative, chaotic, messy, sociable, isolated, imaginative, real, risky, boisterous, silly, peaceful, sometimes even almost silent! (And it is likely to move between different styles rapidly.)

Through play children learn about themselves, the people around them, their environment, their community, and where they fit within that community. Through play too (without realising it), they explore, develop and practice skills they will use throughout their lives. It allows children to be real, creative and inventive. It inspires and motivates.

Play is an integral and essential part of being human.

And how exactly does this help with all-age worship?

In the same way that play unites cultures and abilities, our worship should bring all God's people (of all ages) together with the common purpose of worshipping Him.

Like play, all-age worship should be exciting and compel others to join in! We worship God because we can't help ourselves, it's the overflow of a grateful heart. Worship should be spontaneous, freely chosen, and perhaps even structure-free and wonderfully all-over-the-place?

I'm so passionate about all-age worship, and believe it should give us all (including adults and introverts!) a safe place to be who we are, to figure out how we fit in the body of Christ, and an uplifting forum to worship however we find the most comfortable.

I don't believe that all-age worship is an occasion to be forced into doing actions to songs aimed only at children, nor is it a time to say childish prayers or play silly games.

I believe that we can find inclusive language and sing songs that connect with everyone in all age worship. At BIG Ministries we offer a variety of points of engagement during all-age worship. People will be: singing, doing actions, writing, drawing, dancing, flag-waving, clapping, sitting in silence or even finding space to chat all at the same time! By encouraging spontaneity in worship we allow people to be free to engage with God and worship Him alongside everyone else.

Perhaps like preparing a room for a family party, we should re-think our all-age worship times to incorporate all the different ways we can engage with God, all at the same time?

All-age worship should truly be the play of the Church. All-age worship should allow all ages to be real, creative and inventive in their worship of our massive, creative and very real God even if that becomes 'wonderfully all-over-the-place'! All-age worship, as well as age-specific times of worship, should inspire us as a community of believers and motivate us to go out and change the world in Jesus' name.

Our worship - our play - is an integral and essential part of being human.

Jo Squires
Director of BIG Ministries
www.bigministries.co.uk

69

There is strength within the sorrow

(Sovereign over us)

Key = B

Capo 4 (G)

♩ = 80

Aaron Keyes,
Bryan Brown & Jack Mooring

G♯m(Em)
E(C)
You are work - ing in our wait - ing,
You're the lift - er of the low - ly,
F♯(D)
B(G)
sanc - ti - fy - ing us;
com - pas - sio - nate and kind;
G♯m(Em)
E(C)
when be - yond our un - der - stand - ing,
you sur - round and you up - hold me,
F♯(D)
B(G)
Chorus
You're teach - ing us to trust.
Your plans
and your pro - mi - ses are my de - light.

E(C)
B(G)
F♯(D)
G♯m(Em)
(plans) are still to pros - per,
You've not for-got - ten us, you're
E(C)
B/D♯(G/B)
F♯(D)
with us in the fire and the flood.
E(C)
B(G)
F♯(D)
G♯m(Em)
Last time to Coda
E(C)
F♯(D)
Faith-ful for-e - ver, per-fect in love, you are sov-'reign o - ver us.
1.
D.C.(v.2)
3.,4.
D.S. (al Coda)
B(G)
B(G)
2.
B(G)
Mid section
B(G)
(small note on rpt)
E-ven what the e-ne-my means for e-

E(C)
C♯m7(Am)
- vil, you turn it for our good, you turn it for our
F♯/A♯(D/F♯)
B(G)
good and for your glo - ry. E - ven in the val - ley you are faith -
E(C)
C♯m7(Am)
- ful, you're work - ing for our good, you're work - ing for our
1.
F♯(D)
2.
F♯/A♯(D/F♯)
D.S.
good and for your glo - ry. good and for your glo - ry. Your
Coda
B(G)

There's a place I know where kindness lives

(Atmosphere)

Key = D

♩ = 70

Mark Tedder
& Jordan Riley

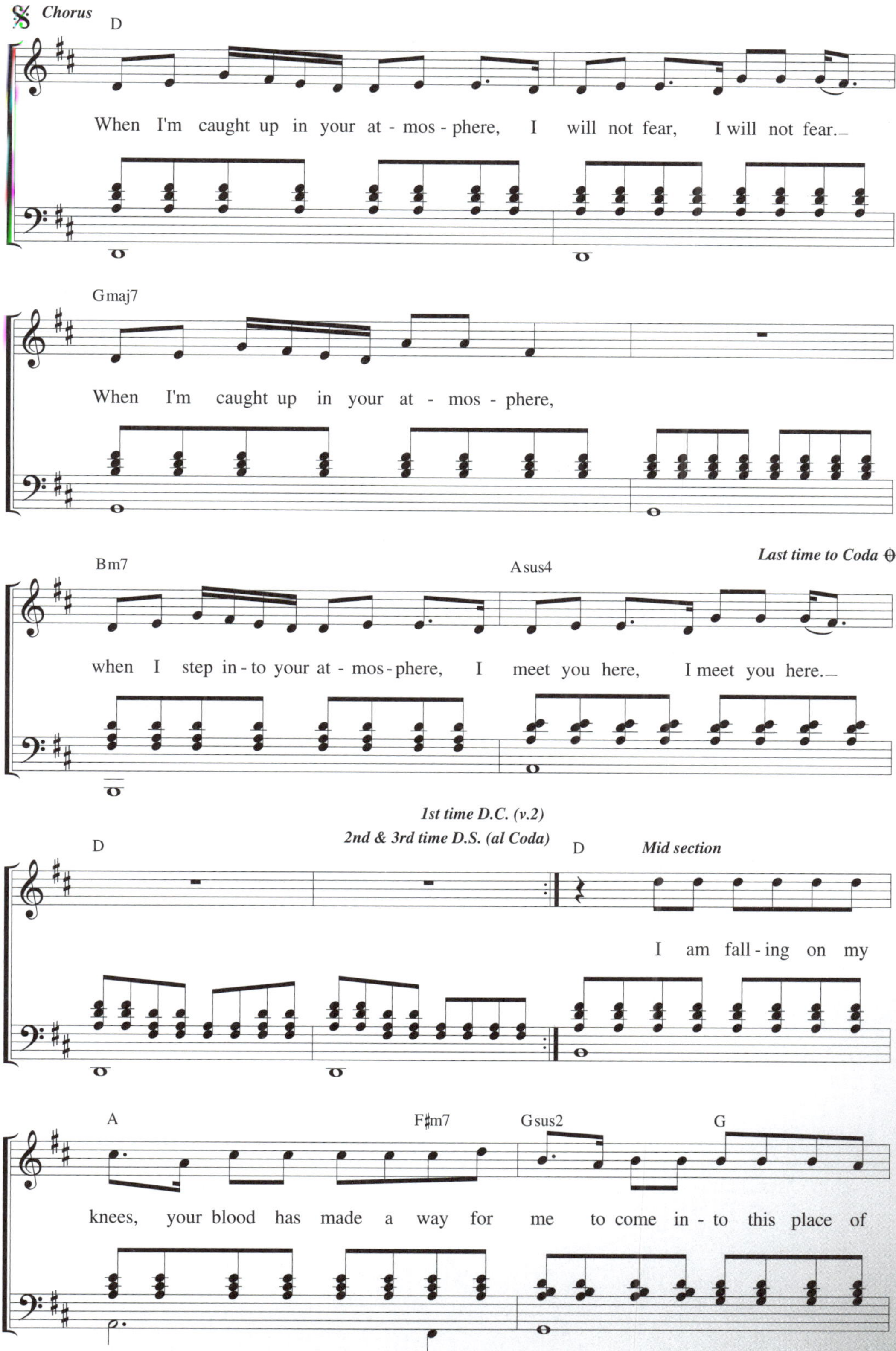
Chorus
D
When I'm caught up in your at - mos - phere, I will not fear, I will not fear.
Gmaj7
When I'm caught up in your at - mos - phere,
Bm7
Asus4
Last time to Coda
when I step in - to your at - mos - phere, I meet you here, I meet you here.
1st time D.C. (v.2)
2nd & 3rd time D.S. (al Coda)
D
D
Mid section
I am fall - ing on my
A
F♯m7
Gsus2
G
knees, your blood has made a way for me to come in - to this place of

G/D D Bm7 A F♯m7
mer - cy. Broke in - to this heart of shame, tore the veil and loosed my
Gsus2 G Asus4
D.S.
chains; I am free to live a - gain.
Coda
G D

There's a song to be sung

(Together)

71

Key = D

Andy Smith

Bm A/C♯ D G A Bm7 D/A Asus4
turn-ing tide. My bro-ther stand - ing here, right by my side.
A Chorus G D Asus4 A
And oh, how beau - ti-ful it is, when we
Bm A G D
love one a-no - ther. And oh, how beau - ti-ful it is
Asus4 A Bm A G
when we ho - nour each o - ther. And oh, we're
D G D
bet-ter to-ge - ther. And so, lets love come-what-e - ver. To-night: -

We really enjoyed recording this song for "The Source: New Songs for the Church"

72 There's a sonnet of love
(My heart is singing loud)

Key = A♭

Capo 1 (G)

Pete James

♩ = 120

Fm(Em)
D♭(C)
E♭(D)
– no-thing could se-pa-rate me___ from___ your love, love, love.
𝄋
A♭(G)
Chorus
E♭/G(D/F♯)
Fm(Em)
D♭(C)
How won - der - ful,___ how mar - vel - lous,_
A♭(G)
Cm(Bm)
Fm(Em)
_ my Sa - viour's love a-bounds, my
D♭(C)
A♭(G)
E♭/G(D/F♯)
heart is sing-ing loud. Ex - tra - va - gant,_
Fm(Em)
D♭(C)
A♭(G)
_ no-thing could e - ver___ com-pare,___ my

Last time to Coda
Cm(Bm)
Fm(Em)
D♭(C)
Sa - viour's love a - bounds, my heart is sing - ing loud.
A♭(G)
1. D.C.
2.
You
Mid section
A♭(G)
love me un - der blue skies. (You love me un - der
love me when the fire burns. (You love me when the
blue skies.) You love me through the dark nights. (You
fire burns.) You love me when the flame dies. (You
Fm(Em)
love me through the dark nights.) You
love me when the flame dies.) Be - fore my life's con -

neither HEIGHT nor DEPTH
nor
ANYTHING ELSE
in all creation
will be able to
separate us
from the love of GOD
that is in CHRIST
JESUS our Lord

ROMANS
8:39

73

This is my revelation

(Beneath the waters (I will rise))

Key = A♭

Capo 1 (G)

♩ = 74

Brooke Ligertwood
& Scott Ligertwood

2.,3.
Fm(Em)
E♭(D)
Chorus
D♭(C)
A♭(G)
I will rise, I will rise, as
E♭(D)
Fm(Em)
D♭(C)
Christ was raised to life. Now in him, now in him
A♭(G)
E♭(D)
Last time to Coda
1. D.C. (v.3.)
2.,4.,5. D.S. (al Coda)
I live. I will rise,
3.
Mid section
D♭(C)
A♭(G)
I rise as you are risen, declare your rule and reign;
Your word it stands e-ter-nal, your King-dom knows no end,
E♭(D)
1.
Fm(Em)
my life con-fess your Lord-ship, and glo-ri-fy your name.
your praise goes on for-e-ver,

2.
Fm(Em)
D♭(C)
and on and on a - gain. No pow'r can stand a - gainst you,
A♭(G)
E♭(D)
no curse as - sault your throne, no one can steal your glo - ry,
Fm7(Em7)
D♭(C)
for it is yours a - lone. I stand to sing your prais - es,
A♭(G)
E♭(D)
Fm7(Em7)
D.S.
I stand to tes - ti - fy, for I was dead in my sin, but now I rise.

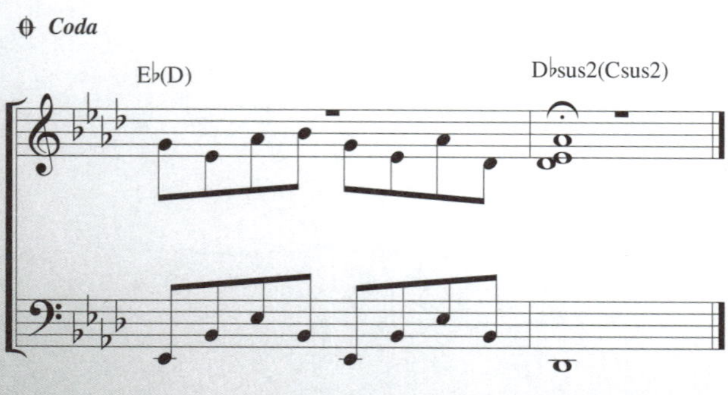
Coda
E♭(D)
D♭sus2(Csus2)

Three days in the grave

(Death is beaten)

74

Capo 3 (D)

♩ = 120

Key = F

Vicky Beeching

Dm7(Bm7) F/A(D/F♯) B♭2(G2)
dark-ness trem-bles at the sight, at the sight. Christ is ri-sen,
D.S. for last chorus repeat (al Coda)
Last time to Coda
F/A(D/F♯) C(A) B♭2(G2) Gm7(Em7) F/C(D/A) C(A)
reign-ing and glo-ri-ous. Christ is ri-sen, for-e-ver vic-to-ri-ous.
1st time D.C. (v.2)
B♭/F(G/D) F(D) Dm7(Bm7) C(A) B♭/F(G/D) F(D) Dm7(Bm7) C(A)
Mid section
Gm7(Em7) F/A(D/F♯)
Like La-za-rus, speak to us, in our graves, say our names,
B♭(G) F/C(D/A) C(A) Gm7(Em7)
and we will walk in-to the light of day. Grave clothes gone, hands held high,

F/A(D/F♯)
3
1.
B♭(G)
C(A)
we lift our voi - ces to the sky, and sing: 'You've made us a - live'.
2.
B♭(G)
Csus4(Asus4)
C(A)
Gm7(Em7)
and sing: 'You've made us a - live, you've made us a - live,
F/A(D/F♯)
B♭(G)
C(A)
D.S.
you've made us a - live'.
Coda
B♭/F(G/D) F(D)
Dm7(Bm7) C(A)
B♭/F(G/D) F(D)
Dm7(Bm7) C(A)

75 Through you I can do anything

(Nothing is impossible)

Key = C

Jonathan Hunt

2nd time to Coda 1
Last time to Coda 2
Fmaj9
C
C/D
thing is im-pos-si-ble,
Fmaj7
F2
C
C/D
Fmaj9
no-thing is im - pos-si-ble,
whoah.
Chorus
C
Dm7+4
F
Am7
I'm not gon-na live by what I see,
I'm not gon-na
Gsus4
F
Am7
Gsus4
live by what I feel,
deep down, I know that you're
F
Am7
Gsus4
here with me,
I know that you can do

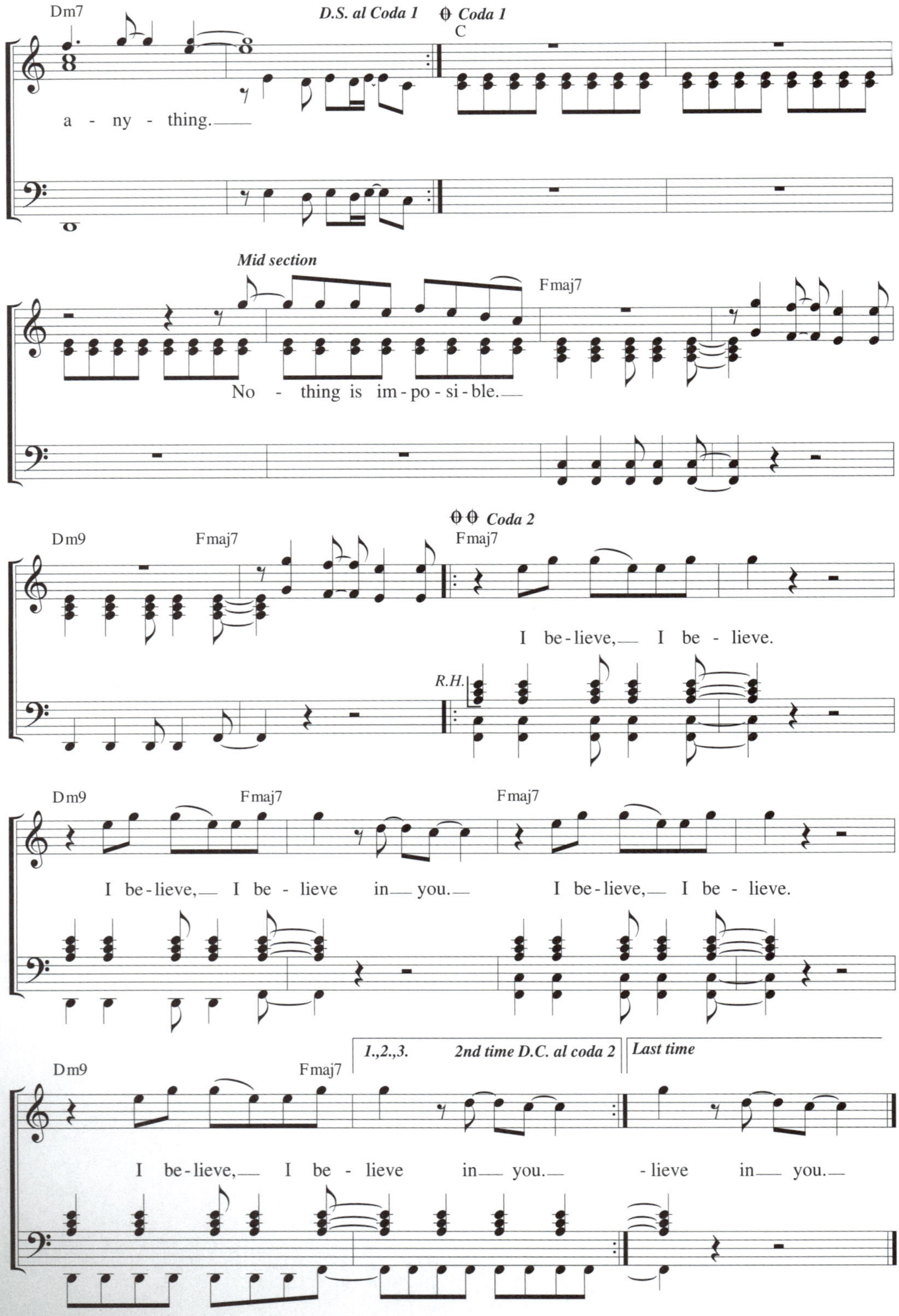
Dm7
D.S. al Coda 1
Coda 1
C
a - ny - thing.
Mid section
Fmaj7
No - thing is im - po - si - ble.
Dm9
Fmaj7
Coda 2
I be - lieve, I be - lieve.
R.H.
I be - lieve, I be - lieve in you.
1.,2.,3.
2nd time D.C. al coda 2
Last time
- lieve in you.

United we stand

(All God's children)

76

Key = G

♩ = 112

Mark Beswick
& Nick Herbert

Chorus
D/F♯
G
Am
to - ge - ther We're (all) God's chil - dren, ar - ri -
Em
C
G
- ving in your arms, be - com - ing who we are. We're all God's chil -
Am
Em
C
- dren, no mat - ter where you're from, u - ni - ted now as one. Woah,
G
Am
Em
woah, we're shin - ing like the stars
C
G
Am
a - bove. Woah, woah, we're shin -

(Fine)
1.
Em C G D
ing like the stars a-bove.
D.C. (v.2)
2.
Em C2 G D Em
C G Mid section D Em
Ev-'ry heart has a part to play.
C G D Em
Ev-'ry heart has a part to play. Ev-'ry heart has a part to play.
1. 2. D.S. al fine
C C
Ev-'ry heart, set a-part, has a part to play. part, has a part. We're all

77 Unshakeable, unmoveable

(Unshakeable)

Key = G

Noel Robinson,
Donna Akodu & Yolanda Antonio

C Em7
Yes, you are wor - thy, your word says I should stand
G7 D/C C D/C C D/C C D/C
and trust you on - ly. What you say keeps me
C Am C/G
be - liev - ing; I wan-na lose my-self my all in you. Un -
1. Fmaj7 D.C.
2.,3. Fmaj7 D.S.
you.
4. Fmaj7
you.

78

Upon a cross, the King of love, he died

(Giving you my all)

Key = A

♩ = 78

Tom Field

D
Bm
Chorus
heart shouts out this song. I'm giv-ing you my all,
A
Bm
D
Lord Je-sus, my all, Lord Je-sus, for you have made a way.
A
E/G♯
A
Bm
You broke ev-'ry chain that held me, now I
Last time to Coda
(Small notes 3rd time)
1.
D
A
E/G♯
dance free-ly, for you have made a way, I'm giv-ing you my
D A E D A E
D.C. (v.2)
all, my all. 2. Now

3.
D.S. al Coda
2.
A
E/G♯
I'm giv-ing you my all,
Mid section
(1st time instrumental)
D
E
1.-4.
A/C♯
I'm giv-ing you my all, I'm giv-ing you my all, all I have is yours..
5.
D.S.
all I have is yours. I'm giv-ing you my all,
Coda
D
A
E
I'm giv-ing you my all, my
1.
2.
Dsus2
all. I'm giv-ing you my

We call out your name in the darkness

(Greater than all)

79

Key = Em

♪ = 160

Autumn Hardman
& Dave Dodgson

Chorus
D
C
G
Our God, our God has done great things,
D
1.,2.,4.
2nd & 3rd times D.S.
C
our God is great - er than all.
Em
Gmaj7
Cmaj7
Em
Gmaj7
Cmaj7
D.C.(v.3)
3.,5.
2nd time jump to
C
than all.
(3rd time)
whoah,
G/B
Em
Gmaj7
Bm
Cmaj7

1.,2.
(2nd time)
Whoah, whoah,
G D G/B Cmaj7 G/B
3.
D
Mid section
C Em7
All of the praise, un-to your name, be lift - ed
D C Em7
Last time to Coda
high - er. All of the praise, un-to your name for - e - ver.
D/F♯ Cmaj7
D.S.
And
R.H.
Coda
D Cmaj7
GOT AN MRL LICENCE FROM CCLI.CO.UK?
THEN YOU'RE ALL SET -
PHOTOCOPY AS MUCH AS YOU NEED!!

80 We were made to see and know

(Son of righteousness)

Key = G

Jules Burt,
Paul Oakley & Pete Coggan

Cmaj9
Gadd2
gin - ning; you are wor - thy, oh!
me; you are wor - thy, oh!
lives; you are wor - thy, oh!
1.
D.C. (v.2)
Cmaj9
G2
2.,3.
Bridge
Cmaj7
Am7
Em
Je - sus, you're the ra - diance of the Fa - ther's glo - ry and
G
Cmaj7
Am
D
love, i - mage of the un - seen One, you are God.
Baug7
Chorus
C
G
You are the song that lives in - side of me, you are the well
that springs e - ter - nal peace, you are the Son

Bm
Em
C
that o - ver - flows with ri - vers of joy;
you are wor - thy, oh!
of right - eous - ness, with heal - ing in your wings.
You are wor - thy, oh!
G
Last time to Coda
D
1.,3.
G/B
You are wor - thy, oh!
You are the hope
You are wor - thy, oh!
2.
D.C.(v.3)
Baug7
4.
D
Mid section
C
(now.) We join with hea - ven,
G
D
G/B
an - gels all a - round, we're ech - o - ing their praise, we wor - ship you
Cmaj9
Gadd2
D
1.
Gadd2/B
now.

I DESIRE TO BE AS JESUS

I desire to be as Jesus,
I want to live my life so that others see Christ in me.
I desire to speak with Jesus' words,
I want to use my words with Christ's wisdom and compassion.
I desire to do Jesus' work,
I want to use my time to bring Christ to my world.

81

Capo 4 (G)

♩ = 126

We're ready at the line looking out

(Running)

Key = B

Matt Crocker
& Scott Ligertwood

2.
G♯m7(Em7)
E(C)
B(G)
E(C)
We're ne-ver gon-na stop, we're ne-ver gon-na stop.
Chorus
G♯m7(Em7)
E(C)
B(G)
E(C)
We are run-ning, chas-
G♯m7(Em7)
E(C)
B(G)
-ing af-ter all that you are. We are run-ning,
2nd & 4th time D.S.S. (al Coda)
Last time to Coda
E(C)
G♯m7(Em7)
E(C)
be-cause all that you are, is all that we want, Lord.
(2.4. that we want. We're)
1.
B(G)
E(C)
G♯m7(Em7)
E(C)
D.C.(v.3)
3. Ev -

2.
C♯m(Am)
E(C)
Bridge
B(G)
F♯(D)
Whoa, whoa, whoa,
C♯m(Am)
E(C)
B(G)
F♯(D)
Mid section
whoa, whoa, whoa. On -
C♯m(Am)
E(C)
B(G)
- wards we draw to-wards your light, des - perate we seek to know you
F♯(D)
C♯m(Am)
E(C)
more and more, fur - ther we look be-yond our - selves to your love,
1.
2.
D.S.S.
B(G)
F♯(D)
F♯(D)
to your love. On - 'Cause we are

Whoa, whoa,
Coda
B(G)
E(C)
G♯m7(Em7)
whoa, whoa. whoa,
E(C)
B(G)
E(C)
whoa.
G♯m7(Em7)
E(C)
B(G)
Rit.

82

What can separate me from your love?

(Power of your love)

Key = C

Noel Robinson
& Donna Akodu

Em/B
Gm/B♭
me, your love that holds me, your love that keeps
F/A
G/B
C
me strong. The pow'r of your love that re-deemed
Em/B
Gm/B♭
me, your love that heals me, your love that re-lea-
F/A
Dm
Em7 Fmaj7
ses love. Your love.
Last time to Coda
Dm
Em7 Fmaj7
Your love.

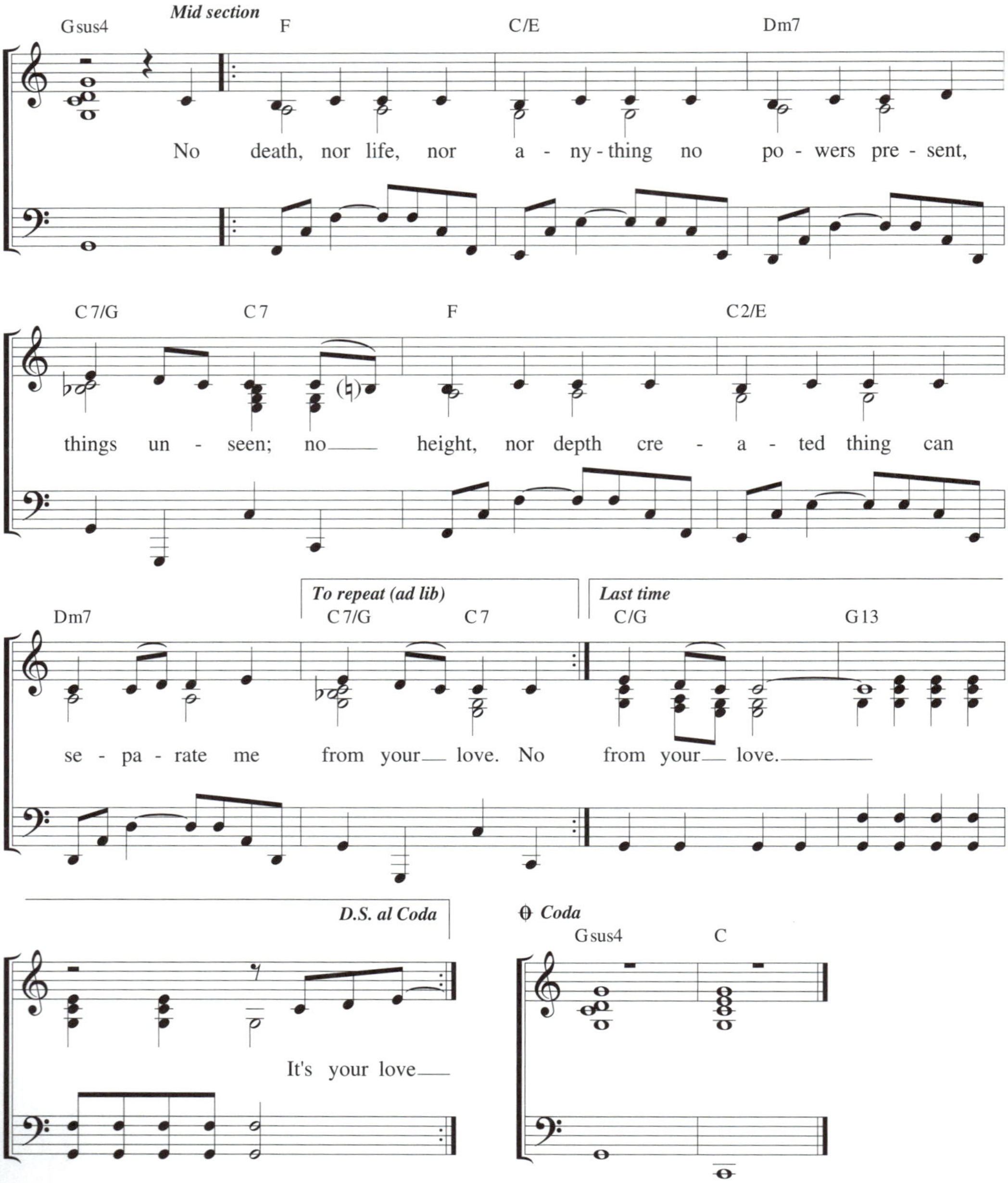
Mid section
Gsus4 F C/E Dm7
No death, nor life, nor a - ny - thing no po - wers pre - sent,
C 7/G C 7 F C2/E
things un - seen; no height, nor depth cre - a - ted thing can
To repeat (ad lib)
Last time
Dm7 C 7/G C 7 C/G G13
se - pa - rate me from your love. No from your love.
D.S. al Coda
It's your love
Coda
Gsus4 C

83

What good are these hands

(Move)

Key = C

Mark Warren,
Joel Warren & Don Chaffer

This song is included on "The Source: New Songs for the Church"

84

What heart could hold the weight of your love?

(Holy)

Key = Bb

Matt Redman, Jonas Myrin & Jason Ingram

Capo 3 (G)

♩ = 70

2.
F(D)
Chorus
Gm7(Em) E♭(C) Fsus4(D) F(D)
You are ho - ly, ho - ly, ho - ly God most
Gm7(Em) E♭(C) Fsus4(D) F(D) Gm7(Em) E♭(C)
high and God most wor - thy. You are ho - ly, ho - ly,
Fsus4(D) F(D) Gm(Em) E♭(C)
1. D.C.(v.2)
Fsus4(D) F(D)
ho - ly, Je - sus, you are, Je - sus, you are. 2. Your name a
2.,4. D.S.
Fsus4(D) F(D)
5.,6.
Fsus4(D) F(D) Gm(Em) E♭(C)
(small notes opt. last time)
You are Je - sus, you are Je - sus, you are.
(Fine)
D.C.(v.3) al fine
F(D)
3.
Fsus4(D) F(D) Gm(Em) E♭(C)
3. And you will Je - sus, you are Je - sus, you are.

Mid section
Fsus4(D) F(D) Fsus4(D) F(D) E♭(C) B♭(G) F(D) Gm(Em)
Who shall we say you are? You're the liv-ing God.
E♭(C) B♭(G) F(D) Gm(Em)
Who shall we say you are? You're the Great I Am.
E♭(C) B♭(G) F(D) Gm(Em) E♭(C) Gm(Em)
The high-est name of all, you're all you say you are.
F(D)
D.S.
You are

G R
THE REBEL'S GUIDE TO
THE GOOD NEWS
CRIS ROGERS

85 When I feel the cold of winter

(Song of Solomon)

Key = C

♩ = 72

Martin Smith

There's a beautiful acoustic arrangement of this song on "The Source: New Songs for the Church".

86 When I'm dry and thirsty Lord

(Your love is everything)

Key = Gm

Capo 3 (Em)

♩ = 92

Chris McClarney,
Anthony Skinner & Mark Woodward

Chorus
E♭(C)
B♭/D(G/B)
Your love heals ev - 'ry di - sease, your love fills my ev - 'ry need,
Gm(Em)
F(D)
your love is ev - 'ry thing to me, your love is ev - 'ry - thing.
E♭(C)
B♭/D(G/B)
Your love heals ev' - ry di - sease, your love fills my ev - 'ry need,
Gm(Em)
1.
Fsus4(Dsus4)
E♭(C)
your love is ev - 'ry - thing your love is ev - 'ry - thing.
Gm(Em) B♭(G) E♭(C) B♭(G) F/A(D/F♯) Gm(Em) B♭(G) E♭(C)
D.C.
When I'm

2.,3.
Mid section
F/A(D/F♯)
E♭(C)
I will not for-get,
(1.-4.) I won't for-get your pro-mi-ses.
(5.,6.) that no-thing is im-pos-si-ble.
F(D)
Gm(Em)
I will not for-get,
I won't for-get your love.
1.,3.,4.,5.
2.
D.S.
6.
I will not for-get
Tag
B♭/D(G/B)
Your love heals ev-'ry di-sease,
your love fills my ev-'ry need,
You're ev-'ry-thing,
you're ev-'ry-thing to me, Je-sus.

When my heart is overwhelmed

(God my rock)

Key = D

♩ = 98

Paul Baloche
& Brenton Brown

Chorus
D
A
1.You are the strength of my heart, you are the strength of my heart,
2.You are the joy of my life, you are my song in the night,
Bm
I can re - ly on you, I can re - ly
there is no one as true, Je - sus I trust
Last time to Coda
1.
D.C. (v.2)
2.,4.,6.
D.S. (ch.2) (al Coda)
G
on you.
in you.
2. When I've
3.,5.
D
A
Yeah!
D/F♯
Bm
G

Don't know this one?
You can hear it on
"The Source: New Songs for the Church".

88 Who breaks the power of sin and darkness

(This is amazing grace)

Key = C

♩ = 100

Josh Farro,
Phil Wickham & Jeremy Riddle

Fmaj9
Am7
that you would take my place,
Gsus4
C
that you would bear my cross.
You would lay down your life,
Last time to Coda
1.
Fmaj9
Am7
Gsus4
That I would be set free;
Je-sus, I sing for all that you've done for me.
D.C.(v.3)
C
Fmaj7
All that you've done for me.
2.
Gsus4
C
All that you've done for me.

Mid section
Fmaj7
C
(2nd time 8va)
Wor - thy is the Lamb who was slain, —
Fmaj7
— and wor - thy is the King - who con - quered the grave. —
Am7
1.
Fmaj7
Wor - thy is the Lamb who was slain, — and wor - thy is the King who
2.
Fmaj7
con - quered the grave. — — wor - thy, wor - thy, wor - thy.
D.S. al Coda
This is a - maz - ing — grace, —
Coda
Gsus4
C
all that you've done for me. —

89

Who has held the oceans in his hands

(Behold our God)

Key = C

♩ = 73

Meghan Baird, Jonathan Baird,
Stephen Altrogge & Ryan Baird

C G/B Am F
hold our King, no-thing can com - pare; come let us a -
D.S. (Last chorus repeat)
Last time to Coda
C G
1. C Em C Em
dore him!
(Be -)
2. F2 Em F2
Him!
Mid section
(Women)
G
3. C C
Let your
Him!
(Men)
You will reign for -
glo - ry fill the earth.
Let your glo - ry fill the earth.
F/C C F/C
e - ver!
You will reign for - e - ver!

– Let your glo - ry fill the earth. Let your
Am7 F Am7
You will reign for - e - ver! You will reign for -
glo - ry fill the earth. Let your glo - ry fill the earth.
F C F
e - ver! You will reign for - e - ver!
D.S. al Coda
– Let your glo - ry fill. Be -
Am7 F
You will reign for - e - ver! Be -

Coda
C
him!

NO LICENCE, NO COPY....
BUT DON'T WORRY – YOU CAN GET AN
MRL LICENCE FROM CCLI.CO.UK

Who is like you Lord in all the earth

(Your presence is heaven)

GRAMMY AWARD BEST CONTEMPORARY CHRISTIAN MUSIC SONG WINNER 2013

Key = Bm

♩= 140

Israel Houghton
& Micah Massey

(v.2)
(v.3 repeat 8va)
Bm7
G
D
Je - sus, you're the cup that won't run dry. Your
hold - er of my fu - ture days to come.
Je - sus, you're the cup that won't run dry.
Chorus
Asus4
G2
D
pre - sence is hea - ven to me.
Asus4
Your pre - sence is
G2
D
1st time D.C. (v.2)
3rd time D.S.
hea - ven to me.
(D.S.) (Lord, your)

Mid section
D
Bm7
Asus4
Oh Je - sus, oh Je - sus, your
G
1.,3.
2.
D.C.(v.3)
pre - sence is hea - ven to me. - ven to me.
4.
Bm7
D
- ven to me.

MATT REDMAN WRITES...

I've been writing worship songs for a couple of decades now and one thing I've realised is that with the subject material we're working with we're never going to run out of ideas or things to say. An old pop music producer once said you can only write four types of songs: I love you, I hate you, go away and come back! I think that's pretty amusing, but the fact is when it comes to worship songs and writing about Jesus and his Kingdom, there's an endless array of things to write and sing about.

Recently I wrote a song called "10,000 Reasons" and what I love most is that this is a huge understatement. If you had a different subject matter, then 10,000 would be a gross exaggeration or overstatement. When it comes to our God, 10,000 is really only just scratching the surface. The Bible contains a song book, the Psalms, with 150 songs. Within those songs are reason after reason to sing the praises of God. We're hearing about his holiness, his kindness, his majesty, his mercy. We're recounting the words of his hands, his signs and his wonders, and his saving ways. The whole of Scripture paints a huge and glorious picture of the One we worship and it does so in fantastic details. So the great news is if you're a Christian worship songwriter you're not starting from scratch. You don't have to make up stories and nothing is a figment of your imagination. All you have to do is feed on the truth and revelation of Jesus as found in the Bible and then let your heart and mind and voice respond out of that. And the key is to try and do that in a passionate, relevant, creative and Scripture honouring way.

John Piper wrote that to sing or speak or paint about breathtaking truth in a boring way is probably a sin. And he's probably right. As worship songwriters, we need to let the love and glory of God light up our life and then fire up our hearts and minds and our imaginations.

Keep writing and singing, for the glory of God.

Matt Redman
www.mattredman.com

LATE BREAKING NEWS!

As this songbook went to the printers,
Matt Redman and Jonas Myrin won the Grammy award
for '**Best Contemporary Christian Music Song**'
for "10,000 Reasons (Bless the Lord)".
You can hear it on **Fresh: New Songs for The Church**.

91 Who is this love amazing?

Key = C

Chris McClarney, John Hartley,
Miriam Webster & Katie Gustafson

♩ = 96

F
C
Gsus4
Am7
- thy, King of glo - ry, King of glo - ry; you're for - e - ver wor -
2° D.S.
Last time to Coda
Chorus
- thy, King of glo - ry, King of glo - ry. O - pen up, o - pen up
(After v.2 D.S. al Coda)
Gsus4
you an - cient gates; o - pen up, o - pen up for the King is com - ing.
D.C.(v.2)
G
Am
Coda
Fmaj7

92

Wrongly accused

(Love has rescued me)

Key = Em

Casey Corum

Bm A G F♯m7 Em7 Em7/D A 7/C♯ A 7 Em7 Em7/D A 7/C♯ A 7
love has res-cued me.
1st time D.C. (v.2)
3rd time D.C. (v.4)
𝄋𝄋 Chorus
Em7 Em7/D A 7/C♯ A 7 Em7 Em7/D A 7/C♯ A 7 Em7 Em7/D A 7/C♯ A 7
(Leader)
1. Your sweet
(2.) A -
(Choir)
1. Your sweet
2. A -
Em7 Em7/D A 7/C♯ A 7 Em7 Em7/D A 7/C♯ A 7
love has re - scued me.
- men.
love has re - scued me.
- men.
Em7 Em7/D A 7/C♯ A 7 Em7 Em7/D A 7/C♯ A 7
I once was
And the church says a -

I once was
A -
Em7 Em7/D A 7/C♯ A 7 Em7 Em7/D A 7/C♯ A 7
blind but now I see.
men.
blind but now I see.
- men.
Em7 Em7/D A 7/C♯ A 7 Em7 Em7/D A 7/C♯ A 7
My sin and
And the church says a -
My sin and
A -
Em7 Em7/D A 7/C♯ A 7 Em7 Em7/D A 7/C♯ A 7
death's been cru - ci - fied.
- men.
death's been cru - ci - fied.
men.
Em7 Em7/D A 7/C♯ A 7 Em7 Em7/D A 7/C♯ A 7
I once was
And the church says a -

I once was
A -
Em7 Em7/D A 7/C♯ A 7 Em7 Em7/D A 7/C♯ A 7
dead, now I'm a - live.
- men.
1.
D.S.(v.3)
dead, now I'm a - live.
Em7 Em7/D A 7/C♯ A 7 N.C.
3. They laid your bo-dy in the grave.
3.
D.S.S.(Ch.2)
dead, now I'm a - live.
Em7 Em7/D A 7/C♯ A 7 Em7 Em7/D A 7/C♯ A 7
And the church says
2.
dead, now I'm a - live. I'm a - live,
Em7 Em7/D A 7/C♯ A 7 Em7
I'm a - live, I'm a - live,

Em7
oh, I'm a - live,
Em7
we're a - live,
we're a - live,
we're a - live.
D.C. (v.5)
4.
oh, we're a - live.
Em7
Em7 Em7/D A 7/C♯ A 7
men.
Mid section
Em7 Em7/G A 7 A 7/C♯ Em7 Em7/G A 7 A 7/C♯
(1st time voice only)
O death, tell me where's your sting, O grave, where's your vic - to - ry?
Play 4 times
Em7 Em7/G A 7 A 7/C♯ Em7 Em7/G A 7 A 7/C♯
Je - sus, ri-sen King; he's a-live and I'm for - gi - ven.
B7(♯9)
Bm A G F♯m7 Em7
Your love, O Lord, your love has res-cued me.

You are my hiding place, within you I will rest

(Hide in you)

♩ = 67

Key = Am

Lara Martin

F Am G F Am
you, a-bide in you, the sha-dow of the Most High is
Last time to Coda
G Am G F C/E
o-ver me. Your ma-je-sty is all I see, the
1.
F C D/F♯ F2
pre-sence of the Most High tak-ing o-ver me: my hid-ing place.
2.
F C Gsus4
2. I pre-sence of the Most High tak-ing o-ver me.
(ad lib repeat)
Mid section
F C Gsus4 F2 C Gsus4 G
You ne-ver

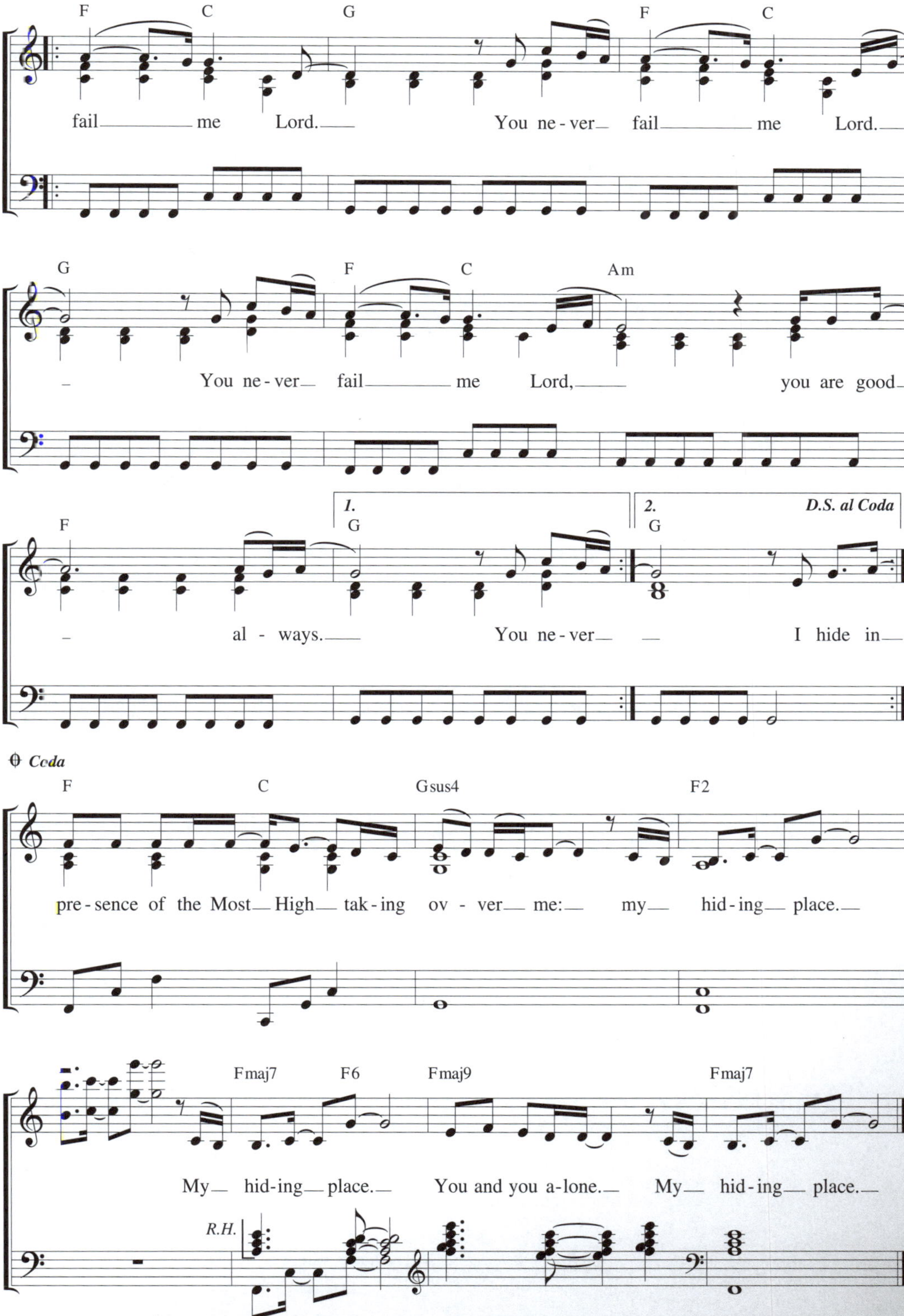
F C G F C
fail me Lord. You ne-ver fail me Lord.
G F C Am
You ne-ver fail me Lord, you are good
F 1. G 2. G D.S. al Coda
al - ways. You ne-ver I hide in
Coda
F C Gsus4 F2
pre-sence of the Most High tak-ing ov - ver me: my hid-ing place.
Fmaj7 F6 Fmaj9 Fmaj7
My hid-ing place. You and you a-lone. My hid-ing place.
R.H.

94 You choose the humble and raise them high

(The same love)

Capo 4 (G)

Key = B

♩ = 102

Paul Baloche
& Michael Rossback

B(G)
F♯(D)
G♯m7(Em7)
- ing us all by name; you are call - ing us all by name.
E2(C2)
B(G)
F♯(D)
The same God that spread the hea - vens wide,
G♯m7(Em7)
E2(C2)
B(G)
the same God that was cru - ci - fied is call - ing us all by name;
F♯(D)
G♯m7(Em7)
1.
E2(C2)
D.C. (v.2)
you are call - ing us all by name.
2.,3.
E2(C2)
F♯(D)
E2(C2)
F♯(D)
G♯m7(Em7)
E2(C2)
Oh, oh, oh, oh.

We're really pleased with the version of this song we recorded for "The Source: New Songs for the Church"...
We hope you like it too!

You draw near

(Faithful)

Capo 3 (D)

♩ = 124

Key = F

Ralph Davis

Bridge
B♭m/D♭(Gm/B♭)
Dm7(Bm7)
B♭(G)
Gra - cious, faith - ful are you
C(A)
1.
2.
Chorus
God. I
B♭(G)
Dm7(Bm7)
Gm(Em)
sing of the Lord's great love for - e - ver, I speak of your faith - ful - ness
F/A(D/F♯)
B♭(G)
F(D)
en - dur - ing. Re - joice in the name a - bove all names:
C(A)
1.
2.
Mid section
Je - sus. We And I am hum - bled

B♭(G)
Dm7(Bm7)
C(A)
(Small notes 3rd time)
here with you.
And I am hum-bled
(Small notes 2nd time)

B♭(G)
Dm7(Bm7)
C(A)
1st time D.C.
2nd time D.S.
here with you.

96 You found me

Key = C♯m

Capo 4 (Am)

Sam Blake & Ian Yates

♩ = 68

We were really excited to have the chance to record this song for "The Source: New Songs for the Church"!

97

You said

Key = G

Kristian Ponsford

♩= 72
G Verse G/B Csus2
1. You said I am beau - ti - ful, won - der - ful - ly made.
2. You said that you knew my name, be - fore I was a - wake.
G G/B Csus2
You said I am ho - ly now, spot - less with - out
You said you can count the hairs up - on this head you
G G/B Csus2
blame. You said I'm a cho - sen one, just as you or - dained.
made. You said I'm worth dy - ing for, if grace is what it takes.
G Csus2 (Repeat v.1) G Chorus
You said, you said. Fa - ther, my ev -
You said, you said.
G/B Csus2 G G/B Csus2
'ry - thing, to your name I'll al - ways cling;

G G/B Csus2 G D 1. G
you are my breath my hope, my life be-gins in you, my
G D Csus2 D.C. (v.2) 2. Csus2 Final Chorus G/B D/F#
life be-gins in you. Fa-ther, my ev-
Em7 Csus2 G/B D/F# Em7 Csus2 G/B D/F#
-'ry-thing, to your name I'll al-ways cling; you are my breath
Em7 Csus2 G/B D/F# Csus2 G/B D/F#
my hope, my life be-gins in you, my life be-gins in you.
Csus2 G/B D/F# Csus2 G
My life be-gins in you.

98 Your blood is the reddest wine

(Communion Song)

Key = D

Andy Smith & Matt Britton

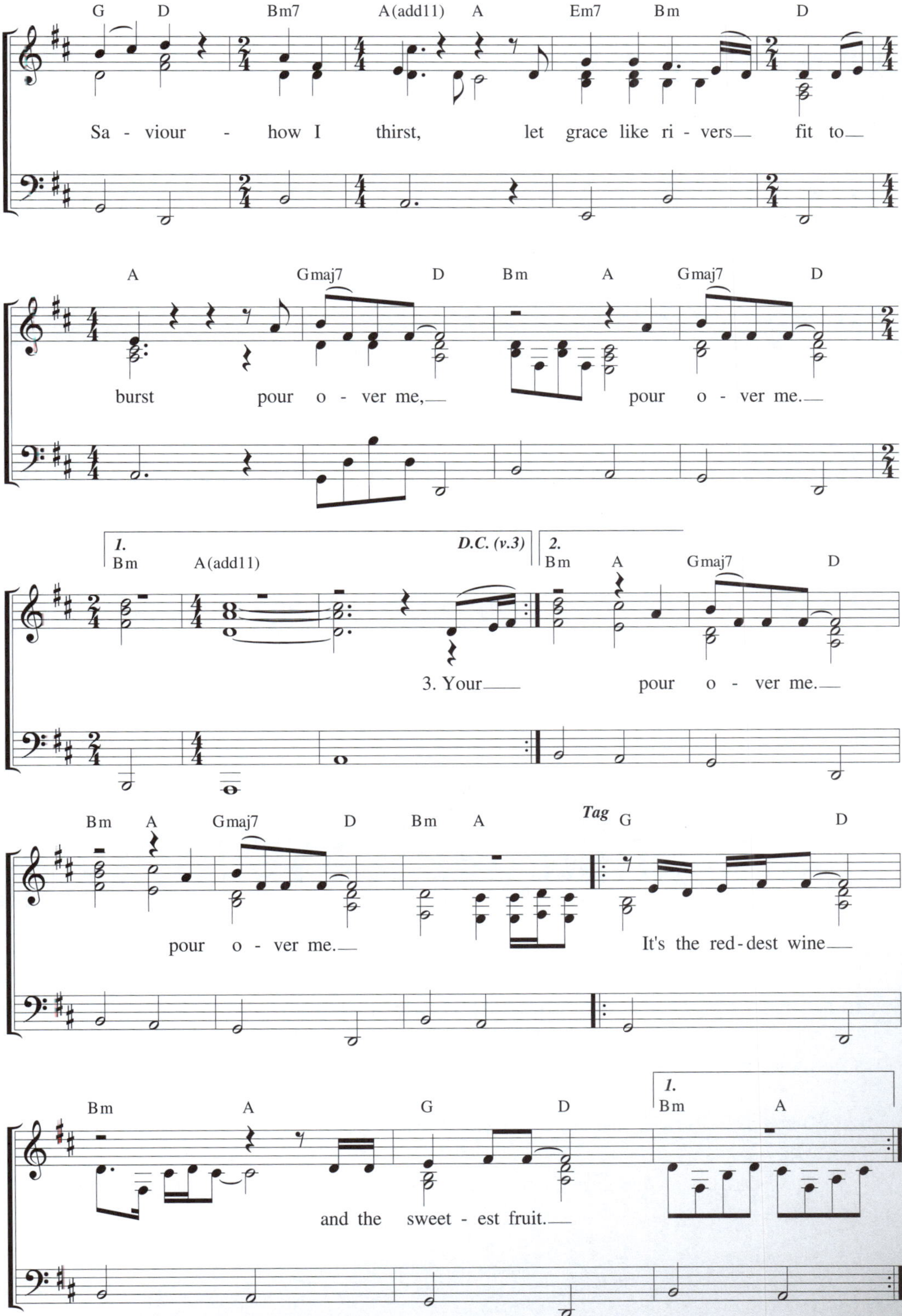
G D Bm7 A(add11) A Em7 Bm D
Sa - viour - how I thirst, let grace like ri - vers fit to
A Gmaj7 D Bm A Gmaj7 D
burst pour o - ver me, pour o - ver me.
1. D.C. (v.3)
Bm A(add11)
3. Your
2.
Bm A Gmaj7 D
pour o - ver me.
Bm A Gmaj7 D Bm A
pour o - ver me.
Tag
G D
It's the red - dest wine
Bm A G D
and the sweet - est fruit.
1.
Bm A

WITNESSING THROUGH LOVE

Jesus, revealed to us in the Gospels and witnessed by the Early Church,
You show us God is love.
Jesus revealed to us in broken bread and wine outpoured,
You show us God is love.
Jesus revealed to us as the bringer of good news and peace,
You show us God is love.
Jesus revealed in new life and transforming power,
You show us God is love.
Help us to live out God's love in all we think, speak and do. Amen.

99 Your love has opened my eyes

(New day)

Key = B

Capo 4(G)

♩ = 160

Ben Cantelon
& Nick Herbert

F♯(D)
F♯sus4(D)
F♯(D)
Chorus
B(G)
It's a new day,
New hope,
it's a new life,
full of your joy,
C♯m(Am)
it's a new
G♯m(Em)
E(C)
4th time to Coda 1
start for ev - 'ry heart that's found you: Je -
1.,3.,5.
To ch.2
2. 6.
B(G)
- sus, we've found you. - sus, we found you.
C♯m(Am)
G♯m(Em)
Whoa, whoa,

Last time to Coda 2
E(C)
whoa.
G♯m(Em)
Verse
E(C)
B(G)
2. We have been healed and re - stored, ev - 'ry -
F♯(D)
G♯m(Em)
E(C)
D.S.(v.2)
thing we are is yours, we'll shine for you.
Coda 1
B(G)
Bsus4(G)
B(G)
Bsus4(G)
- sus, we found you. We found you.
B(G)
Bsus4(G)
B(G)
Mid section
E(C)
B(G)
Light the way, you

F♯(D)
G♯m(Em)
E(C)
B(G)
lead me in your per - fect ways; I'm not a - fraid, you're with
F♯(D)
E(C)
B(G)
G♯m(Em)
me. Light the way, with you it is a
F♯(D)
E(C)
B(G)
F♯(D)
bright - er day; I'm not a - fraid, you're with me.
B(G)
D.S.S. al Coda 2
Coda 2
It's a new
E(C)
E2(C)

100

You're not a God created by human hands

(You are God alone)

Key = G(A♭)

William Matt McDowell

G D/F♯
from be-fore time be-gan, you were on your throne,
Em D C G
you are God a-lone. And right now, in the good times and bad,
D/F♯ Em D 1. C
you are on your throne, you are God a-lone.
D.C. (v.2)
G Bm7 Cmaj7 G Bm7 Am7 G Bm7 Cmaj7 C D Em D/F♯
2. Mid section
(Leader)
C You're un-change-a-ble, G un-shak-a-ble,
(Choir)
You're un-change-a-ble, un-shak-

un - stop - pa - ble, that's who you are.
D/F♯ Em D
- a - ble, un - stop - pa - ble, that's who you are.
Chorus
C E♭7 A♭
You are God a - lone, from be - fore time be - gan,
you were on your throne, you are God a - lone.
Fm E♭ D♭ E♭ A♭
And right now, in the good times and bad,
E♭aug Daug D♭aug Caug C Fm7 E♭/G A♭ D♭
you are on your throne, you are God a - lone.

CHORD BRIDGES TO C

From F

From G

From B♭

From D

CHORD BRIDGES TO D

From F

From G

From B♭

From C

CHORD BRIDGES TO E

From G

From A

From C

From D

CHORD BRIDGES TO F

From D

Dmaj7
B♭/C
C7
F

From G

G
Csus4
C7
F

From B♭

B♭
Gm7
Csus4
C
F

From C

C
C/B
Am
Gm
C7
F

CHORD BRIDGES TO G

From D

From F

From B♭

From C

GUITAR CHORD CHARTS

A good chord vocabulary is essential for a guitarist to feel confident when playing in worship, especially when the situation may involve reading a previously unseen piece of music or picking up a song quickly by ear. The chords on these pages are arranged in 'families' according to key. This is a beneficial way of remembering chords as most songs stick to these groupings. For each key, the first row shows the simplest form of each chord and the second line gives a more interesting substitution. The third line shows the chords most commonly used by guitarists derived by keeping some sort of pedal tone ringing in each chord and the fourth line shows inverted chords with an alternate bass note.

Also included are the Roman Numerals and Nashville Numbers associated with each chord. If you've not come across these before, they are simply an easy way of numbering each chord within a key. This is useful as it means you can take any chord progression in one key and instantly transpose it to another. Furthermore you can try out any of the chords in each column that corresponds to the relevant Roman Numeral and see if there is chord type or inversion which still fits but adds a different flavour. Experimentation like this may open up creative chord progressions that serve as a catalyst to help you to worship in fresh ways or to write new songs.

	Roman	I	II	III	IV	V	VI	VII
	Nashville	1	2	3	4	5	6	7
Key of C	3-note chord (triad)	C 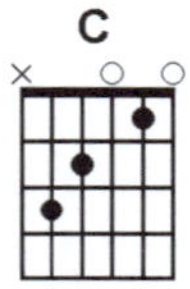	Dm 	Em 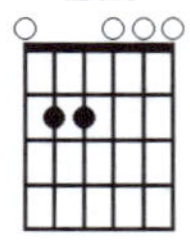	F 	G 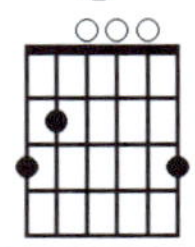	Am 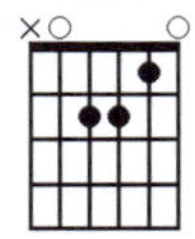	Bdim 
	4-note chord	Cmaj7 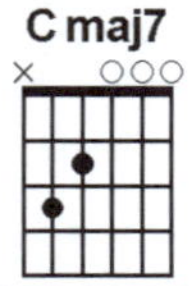	Dm7 	Em7 	Fmaj7 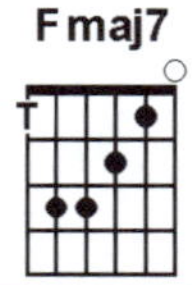	G7 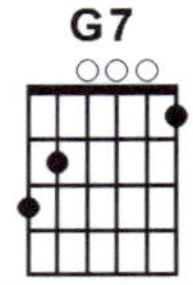	Am7 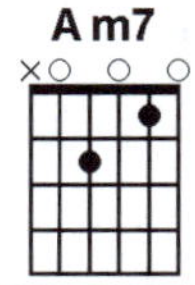	Bm7♭5 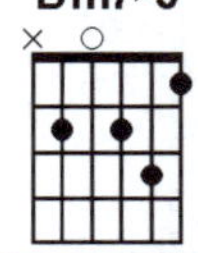
	Alternative substitute	C 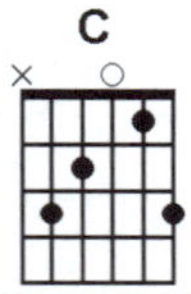	D7sus4 	Em7 	Fsus2 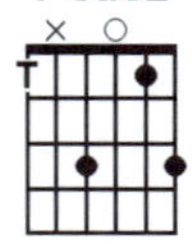	G5 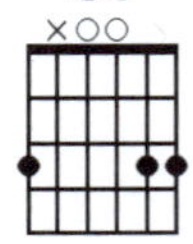	Am7 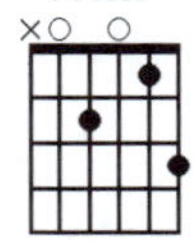	Dsus4/B 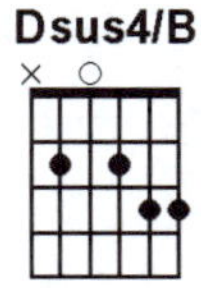
	Alternative bass note	C/E 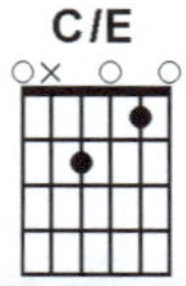	Dm/F 	Em/G 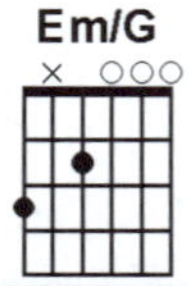	F/A 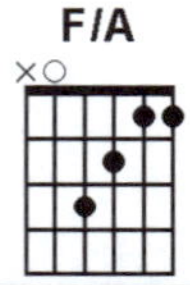	F/G 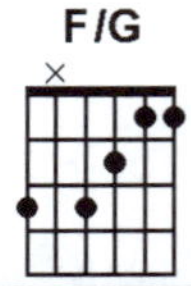	Am/E 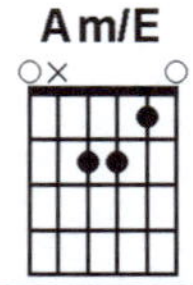	

For all chords in the key of C# or Db, use the chords from the key of C with capo 1

	Roman	I	II	III	IV	V	VI	VII
	Nashville	1	2	3	4	5	6	7
Key of D	3-note chord (triad)	D	Em	F♯m	G	A	Bm	C♯dim
Key of D	4-note chord	Dmaj7	Em7	F♯m7	Gmaj7	A7	Bm7	C♯m7♭5
Key of D	Alternative substitute	Dsus2	Em9	F♯m7	G6sus2	A7sus4	Bm11	Aadd9/C♯
Key of D	Alternative bass note	D/F♯	Em/B	F♯m/A	G/B	G/A	Bm/F♯	

For all chords in the key of D♯ or E♭, use the chords from the key of D with capo 1

		I	II	III	IV	V	VI	VII
Key of E	3-note chord (triad)	E	F♯m	G♯m	A	B	C♯m	D♯dim
Key of E	4-note chord	Emaj7	F♯m7	G♯m7	Amaj7	B7	C♯m7	D♯m7♭5
Key of E	Alternative substitute	E5	F♯m11	G♯madd♭6	Aadd9	Badd4	C♯m7	D♯alt
Key of E	Alternative bass note	E/G♯	F♯m/C♯	G♯m/D♯	A/C♯	A/B	C♯m/G♯	

For all chords in the key of F, use the chords from the key of E with capo 1

For all chords in the key of F# or Gb, use the chords from the key of E with capo 2

	Roman	I	II	III	IV	V	VI	VII
	Nashville	1	2	3	4	5	6	7
Key of G	3-note chord (triad)	G	Am	Bm	C	D	Em	F♯dim
Key of G	4-note chord	Gmaj7	Am7	Bm7	Cmaj7 (3-)	D7	Em7	F♯m7♭5
Key of G	Alternative substitute	G	A7sus4	Dsus4/B	Cadd9	Dsus4	Em7	G/F♯
Key of G	Alternative bass note	G/D	Am/C	Bm/D	C/G	C/D (3-)	Em/G	
	For all chords in the key of G♯ or A♭, use the chords from the key of G with capo 1							
Key of A	3-note chord (Triad)	A	Bm	C♯m (4-)	D	E	F♯m	G♯dim
Key of A	4-note chord	Amaj7	Bm7	C♯m7	Dmaj7	E7	F♯m7	G♯m7♭5 (3-)
Key of A	Alternative substitute	Asus2	Bsus4	C♯m7	D6sus2	Eadd9	F♯m11	Eadd9/G♯
Key of A	Alternative bass note	A/E	Bm/F♯	C♯m/E (4-)	D/A	D/E	F♯m/A	

For all chords in the key of A# or Bb, use the chords from the key of A with capo 1

For all chords in the key of B, use the chords from the key of A with capo 2

SCRIPTURE INDEX

22:37 Love the Lord with all your heart
24:35 The word of God is light in my darkness
26:26 Jesus we come to your table
26:26 Your blood is the reddest wine
27:35 Outside the city walls
27:50 Upon a cross, the King of love, he died
28:2 Come, join the celebration
28:6 How can it be, the One who died
28:7 Three days in the grave
28:20 In my weakness I will come

MARK

10:27 Through you I can do anything
10:27 When I'm dry and thirsty Lord
12:30 Love the Lord with all your heart
13:31 The word of God is light in my darkness
14:22 Jesus we come to your table
14:22 Your blood is the reddest wine
15:22 Outside the city walls
15:37 Upon a cross, the King of love, he died
16:4 Come, join the celebration
16:6 How can it be, the One who died
16:6 Three days in the grave

LUKE

1:49 We call out your name in the darkness
1:52 You choose the humble and raise them high
4:18 In your presence there is fullness of life
4:18 The Kingdom of our God is near
4:18 The Spirit of the Sovereign Lord
4:19 I have tasted of your favour
7:37 Covered in shame, hiding my face
10:27 Love the Lord with all your heart
11:2 Come set your rule and reign
11:2 Even when the waters rise
11:2 For every wounded and broken soul
11:2 Hallowed be your name
11:2 King of love and grace
11:2 Since the dawn of all creation
15:6 I was lost, you took me in
18:27 Through you I can do anything
21:33 The word of God is light in my darkness
22:19 Jesus we come to your table
22:19 Your blood is the reddest wine
23:33 Outside the city walls
23:46 Upon a cross, the King of love, he died
24:2 Come, join the celebration
24:6 How can it be, the One who died
24:6 Three days in the grave

JOHN

1:1 In times of waiting
1:5 Light in my darkness
1:5 Upon a cross, the King of love, he died
1:29 Jesus we come to your table
1:36 Jesus we come to your table
3:16 Outside the city walls
3:16 What can separate me from your love?
3:16 Who breaks the power of sin and darkness
4:10 I've got a river of living water
7:38 I've got a river of living water
8:12 In the midst of the darkness
8:12 It's always like springtime with you
8:12 Outside the city walls
9:5 In the midst of the darkness
9:5 It's always like springtime with you
9:5 Outside the city walls
9:25 Here I'm standing with the rain on my face
10:11 Oh God of power, living word
11:1 Covered in shame, hiding my face
11:43 Three days in the grave
12:3 Covered in shame, hiding my face
12:46 In the midst of the darkness
12:46 It's always like springtime with you
14:3 What heart could hold the weight of your love
14:26 In times of waiting
14:28 What heart could hold the weight of your love
15:5 Lord I desire to live as one
15:26 In times of waiting
19:18 Outside the city walls
19:30 Upon a cross, the King of love, he died
20:1 Come, join the celebration

ACTS

2:3 I feel the heat is rising
3:19 Hope fills my soul
3:21 It's always like springtime with you
4:12 Only one name
9:10 Here I am
10:36 If faith can move the mountains
15:11 Grace, you've shown me grace
16:25 As I go
16:26 Hope fills my soul

ROMANS

5:13 When I'm dry and thirsty Lord
8:26 In my weakness I will come
8:31 As I go
8:34 How can it be, the One who died
8:34 Three days in the grave
8:38 What can separate me from your love?
8:39 Nothing can separate
8:39 There's a sonnet of love
9:26 United we stand
12:1 Here I am
12:1 What good are these hands
12:18 There's a song to be sung
15:9 Sing, north to the south

1 CORINTHIANS

1:9 Jesus you are our everything
2:13 What good are these hands
7:15 There's a song to be sung
9:24 Come set your rule and reign
9:24 Praise you in the morning
9:24 We're ready at the line looking out
10:13 In the midst of the darkness
10:13 Jesus you are our everything
11:23 Jesus we come to your table
11:23 Your blood is the reddest wine
12:9 Faith is rising in this place
13:2 If faith can move the mountains
13:7 Nothing can separate
13:12 Love set me free
13:12 Praise you in the morning
13:12 Who is like you Lord in all the earth
15:52 My hope is built on nothing less
15:55 How can it be, the One who died
15:55 Three days in the grave
15:55 Wrongly accused
15:57 Even when the waters rise
15:58 Unshakeable, unmoveable

2 CORINTHIANS

EPHESIANS

PHILIPPIANS

COLOSSIANS

2 THESSALONIANS

1 TIMOTHY

2 TIMOTHY

HEBREWS

JAMES

1 PETER

2 PETER

1 JOHN

JUDE

REVELATION

THEMATIC INDEX

GOD, LORD AND FATHER (CONTINUED)

GOD'S LOVE AND FAITHFULNESS

GUIDANCE AND DIRECTION

HEALING

HEART WORSHIP

HEAVEN AND THE PROMISE OF ETERNITY

HOLY SPIRIT

JESUS - CROSS AND RESURRECTION

JUSTICE

LOVE AND DEVOTION

MERCY, GRACE AND FORGIVENESS

MISSION

MYSTERY/ TRANSCENDENCE AND POWER OF GOD

PRAISE AND THANKSGIVING

PRAYER AND INTERCESSION

PROCLAMATION

SPOKEN WORSHIP INDEX